The Archaeology of the Kansas Monument Site

A Study in Historical Archaeology on the Great Plains

Rick L. Roberts

DIGDOC BOOKS

Oklahoma City

2014

Library of Congress Control Number: 2014912210

ISBN: 150015444X
ISBN-13: 978-1500154448

FORWARD TO THE 2014 EDITION

This edition contains the full text and illustrations of my original 1978 masters thesis. The content was reformatted for publishing but otherwise remains unchanged, except for minor grammatical and typographic corrections and a few upgrades to some of the graphics. Every effort has been made to insure that text and data were accurately converted. Any errors resulting from the conversion are the author's responsibility.

Like the materials described herein, this book too, is an artifact. The 1970's were a time of theoretical foment in American archaeology. Practitioners of the "new" archaeology were still relatively new themselves. Culture history vs. "processual" archaeology was a very real and lively debate. Historical archaeology was shedding its "handmaiden to history" persona and asserting itself as a legitimate specialty within anthropology. Much of the front matter to the meat of this book addressed these matters through my own perspectives. A 21st Century reader may find some of the arguments almost quaint or self-evident. However, at the time, I was, to the best of my knowledge, the only fulltime historical archaeology specialist between the Mississippi River Valley and California. Defending my chosen profession was a very real concern.

For almost 40 years I have wanted to release my thesis as a book to a broader audience. With the renewed attention the Kansas Monument Site is receiving and the ready availability of ebook and new printing technologies, the time seemed propitious. I want to thank my wife, Kathy, for allowing me to spend a large part of my first year in retirement making that dream come true. To her, my parents, who made the original possible, and to the memory of my mentor, Dr. Carlyle S. Smith, this electronic edition is dedicated.

Rick L. Roberts

Oklahoma City

June 12, 2014

CONTENTS

FIGURES

TABLES

ACKNOWLEDGMENTS

A project such as this thesis could never be the product of a single individual. Throughout the course of my work, I have benefitted from the wise counsel, intellectual challenges, and well-intentioned pep talks of faculty, friends and relatives. To my committee, Dr. Carlyle S. Smith, chairman; Dr. Robert Squier; and Dr. Alfred Johnson, I owe a great debt of gratitude for their good advice and editorial suggestions. Dr. Roger Grange of the University of South Florida gave freely of his time and knowledge. The Merwin Fund of the University of Kansas Endowment Association provided valuable financial support during the research and production of this thesis. Mr. Thomas A. Witty of the Kansas State Historical Society and Mr. Gayle Carlson of the Nebraska State Historical Society provided data integral to this thesis. My friends and colleagues, Ken Brown, Marie Klon, and Chris Wright, all share in the successful completion of this thesis through critical readings of the drafts, pertinent suggestions, and the lending of a helping hand when it was needed. The illustrations included herein add tremendously to the quality of this work due to the talents of Sherry Busbee, photographer; Jean Colglazier, artist; and, most importantly, Patricia Renjifo, my artistic advisor and friend, who is responsible for 90% of the artwork. To all of the faculty and graduate students I have not mentioned, who have tolerated me during my painful metamorphosis from a dedicated Southerner to a Plains archaeologist, I say thank you.

The final people who deserve mention have nothing to do with archaeology. They did not provide data nor did they constructively criticize this report. What they did do was provide support—financial, physical, and emotional—when it was needed. Not once have they let me down when I needed them. Without their constant encouragement and indescribable displays of concern throughout a very difficult period, this thesis may never have been finished. These two very special people are my parents, Mr. and Mrs. Spencer Roberts. It is to them that I respectfully and humbly dedicate this thesis.

1

INTRODUCTION AND BACKGROUND

Europeans began to explore what are now called the Great Plains shortly after the rediscovery of the New World. Coronado was the first to enter the area in 1541. It was not, however, until later in the 18th and, primarily, the 19th centuries, that detailed accounts by explorers and missionaries of encounters with the native populations were produced. The Pawnee are considered among the best-known groups on the Central Plains. Modern investigators of the Pawnee archaeologically have identified many villages, visited and recorded by explorers after 1800.

One of the villages that has received a large amount of attention in discussions of the Pawnee is the Kansas Monument site, 14RP1. This site, which is on the periphery of the area inhabited by the Pawnee (Compare Wedel 1936, Map 1; Grange 1968, Figure 4; This paper Figure 1), has been the subject of debate, debacle, and vehement state pride, e.g., "The War Between Nebraska and Kansas" (Sheldon 1927). Its existence has been known since before the turn of the century. A monument was erected at the site in 1901 (hence, its name) and the area was made a state park. It was 1949 before the site was scientifically investigated (Smith 1949).

Figure 1. The Historic Pawnee Region.

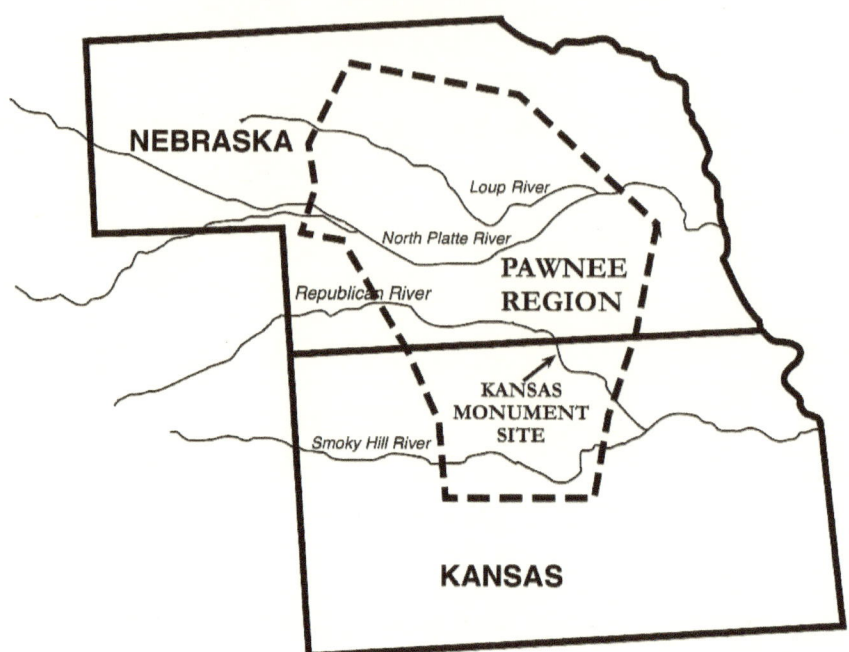

Since that archaeological investigation, various parts of the assemblage have been described and published (Smith 1949, 1950a, and 1950b). Subsequent to this activity, other excavations were undertaken at the site in 1965, 1966, and 1967 (Witty 1967). Despite the considerable amount of activity that has centered on the Kansas Monument site, no one has yet synthesized the available data and adequately assessed the role and position of the site in Pawnee cultural development. The present study seeks not only to draw together the pertinent information but also to effect some explanation of those data. In particular, the data will be examined to determine the site's contribution to the understanding of the changes the Pawnee went through.

LOCATION AND CURRENT STATUS OF THE SITE

The Kansas Monument site is located in the NE¼, Sec. 3, T2S, R5W, Republic County, Kansas. It occupies approximately 12 acres at the top of a promontory on the south bank of the Republican River, a few hundred yards from the river's present edge (Figure 2). Prior to modern developments in the area, the Pawnee inhabitants would have had an almost totally unobstructed 360-degree overview of the surrounding terrain. This, combined with the fact that the site was positioned so that the bluffs along the Republican formed its eastern boundary, suggests the village was well positioned for defensive purposes. The town of Republic lies one mile north and one and one-half miles east of the site.

Figure 2. The Kansas Monument Site.

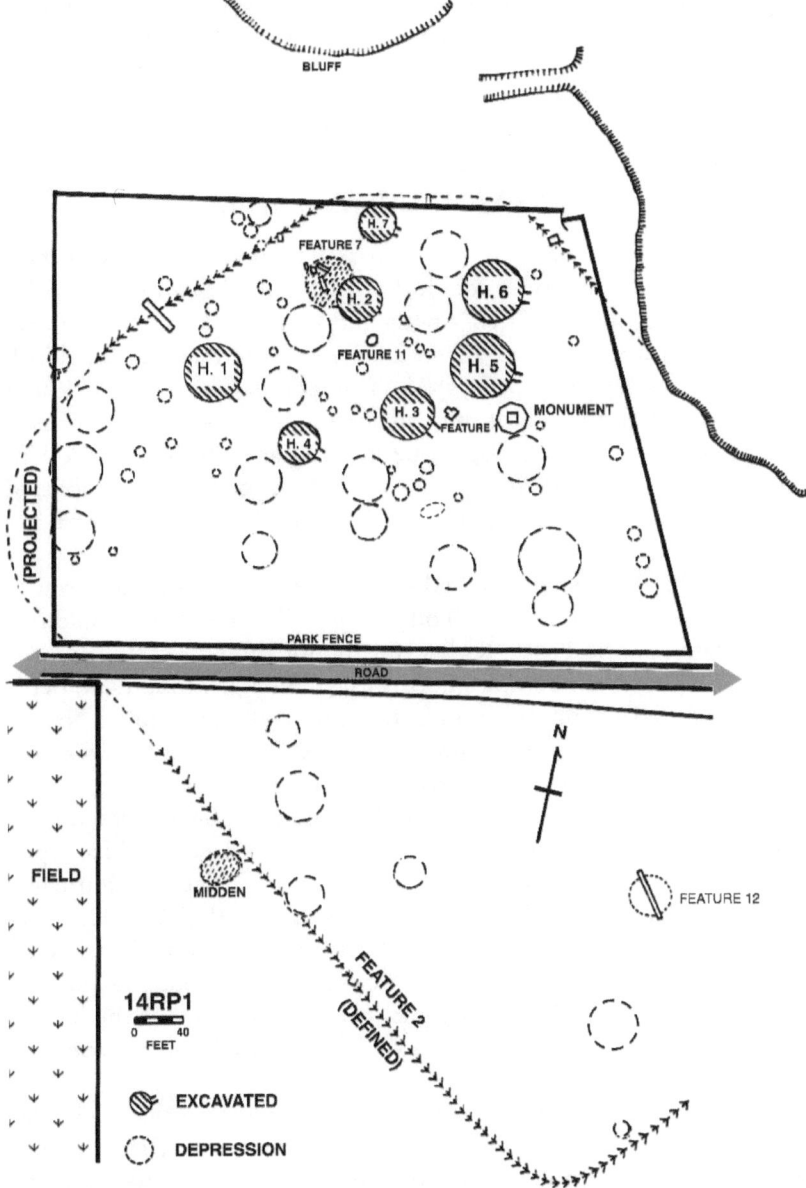

Currently, most of the site, which probably contained in excess of 30 earthlodges during occupation (Wedel 1936:33; Smith 1949:5), is owned by the State of Kansas. It was a gift to the state from the landowner, Mrs. George Johnston, with the stipulation that the land be set aside as a park. This was done and the site is now the location of the Pawnee Indian Village Museum. The state has enclosed with a fence and protected, in whole or in part, 22 earthlodge circles (A museum was built over one of the house circles. The Kansas State Historical Society excavated this house, House 5, and the artifacts were left *in situ*.).

ARCHAEOLOGICAL AND HISTORICAL IMPORTANCE OF THE KANSAS MONUMENT SITE

One of the prime reasons the Kansas Monument site has been the object of so much attention through the years is the legend with which it is associated. It has been storied among the locals of Republic County for many years that it was the site of the Pawnee village that Lt. Zebulon Pike visited during his explorations in 1806. The monument erected in 1901 was intended, "To mark the site of the Pawnee Republic, where Lieut. Zebulon M. Pike caused the Spanish flag to be lowered and the flag of the United States to be raised, September 29, 1806" (Inscribed on the monument, Dunbar 1908:5). Unfortunately this claim is based more on regional hopes and pride than historical fact.

Much ink has been spilled over the controversy as to whether or not this was the village that Pike visited. Today most will agree that it could not be this important historical site. Rather, this honor should rightfully go to the Hill site (25WT1) about 30 miles northwest of Kansas Monument, between the towns of Red Cloud and Guide Rock in Webster County, Nebraska. This latter site was located and purchased by A. T. Hill who was dissatisfied with the identification of the Kansas Monument site as being the Pike-Pawnee village (Hill 1927:162-7). The Hill site is closer to the geographic location and more similar to the description of the village that Pike reported visiting than the Kansas site, which "tallies in nowise with the journals and maps of the expedition" (Wedel 1936:33). Munday (1927:168-92) provides an interesting summary of the historical evidence for the Hill site. George Moorehouse (1927:226-54) defended the Kansas case, but the evidence is simply not strong enough and in some instances borders on the ludicrous. Part of the concern of this thesis is to settle once and for all the controversy over the location of the Pike-Pawnee village.

The question of the Pike visit has given the site historical significance, but it has an archaeological importance that transcends that consideration alone. The Kansas Monument site represents one of two identifiable Pawnee sites within the State of Kansas. It therefore has significance as one of the southernmost known sites of the Pawnee (see Figure 1). It should be noted that there have been reports of other Pawnee sites in Kansas but none of these have been documented archaeologically.

Of additional archaeological importance is the site's position in time. Depending upon the particular reference consulted, Kansas Monument dates from between 1775 and 1831 (Grange 1968:130, 1974:326; Wedel 1936:32-33, 1959:59, 535, 616; Smith 1950a: 2). The exact date will be dealt with later. The significance of these dates is that they represent a time span during which the Pawnee were undergoing the destructive impact of Euro-American culture. Trade goods were supplanting their aboriginal counterparts and the native-made components of the Pawnee material culture were declining in quantity and quality (Wedel 1961:122). Thus, a study of the Kansas Monument site can provide valuable information for the investigation of the impact of "trade culture" on aboriginal behavior. The geographic location of the site offers an even more unique opportunity in that it is an area where not only American but also English, French and Spanish traders were operating as well. So, possibly the archaeological record will provide documentation as to how the material culture of the Pawnee was affected by European and American trade cultures, and how these intrusive cultures interacted with each other in regard to the native culture.

PREVIOUS WORK

Dr. Carlyle S. Smith for the University of Kansas (Smith 1949) conducted scientific excavation at the site in 1949. The material recovered during those six weeks of fieldwork form the substantive basis of this paper. Smith was drawn to the site because it was one of the few villages possibly identifiable with the Republican band of the Pawnee and because he felt that the site was late enough in time to provide a sizable inventory of trade goods. The wealth of artifacts at the site had been revealed earlier by a number of investigators, notably A. T. Hill and Floyd Schultz. Prior to Smith's work, the site had been popular with relic collectors for a number of years. This was particularly true after a township road bisected the site, destroying two houses. The Nystrom collection, donated by one of these early collectors to the University of Kansas, includes several artifacts that may be important in the final analysis of the site.

Smith concentrated on exposing two earthlodge floors (Features 3 and 6) and testing other parts of the site, particularly the fortification wall that surrounded the village and some of the approximately 50 visible cache pits within the village. The artifact assemblage is predominately composed of trade goods.

After 1949 the site was untouched, except for vandals, until 1965 when

Thomas A. Witty, State Archaeologist, excavated an additional portion for the Kansas State Historical Society. Subsequent excavations in 1966 and 1967 by him resulted in eight additional houses being exposed or tested. This work was done as part of the museum building project at the site. In addition, Witty was able to locate and examine eight burials near the site. Vandals had disturbed all of these burials (Witty 1967:218). A sample of the rim sherds recovered by Witty will be used in a later section. The Kansas State Historical Society will describe the remainder of Witty's material in a future publication.

A RESEARCH MODEL FOR THE KANSAS MONUMENT SITE

The preceding pages were devoted to explaining the importance of the site and to providing some background data. These final introductory pages will explain the form of the remainder of this work.

As in any project, this endeavor has undergone many changes since it was begun. In some instances the data were not complete enough to sustain investigation along certain lines. In other instances, the data had completely disappeared. These are the problems one faces when working with an old collection and they have had a direct effect on the final form of this project Basically, there are three approaches operating within this investigation. These approaches can be considered to follow a hierarchical arrangement as follows:

(1) During the course of the investigation, it became painfully obvious that whereas the Pawnee are considered to be among the best known peoples on the Plains and although there have been many archaeological investigations of their sites, there is a paucity of published material on the archaeology of the Pawnee. Therefore, in order to aid in rectifying this situation, the artifacts and features from the Kansas Monument site will be described in detail so that other researchers may have access to this information. The descriptive process will include comparing the material with the artifacts from other sites in order to attempt to identify where the trade material was coming from.

(2) The site will be assigned as definite a date as possible. There are several problems that can benefit from an accurate date. First, it may be possible to end the debate over site's role in the Pike-Pawnee controversy. Secondly, an accurate date will clarify whether this is the site visited by Jedediah Smith in 1826. In addition, a true date for the site will be important in assessing Grange's Lower Loup-Pawnee ceramic seriation (Grange 1968, 1974) as a valid chronological indicator.

(3) The most important aspect of the present work is placing the Kansas Monument site in a broader perspective. This will be accomplished by developing a site seriation, a behavioral model that allows inferences to be

made about changes in Pawnee culture. It will be a model that can be used for collections that have been accumulated over the years but it will be equally applicable to collections obtained in modern excavations. In this way, as data from other sites in the Lower Loup - Historic Pawnee continuum are compared, archaeologists will be able to make behavioral inferences.

HYPOTHESES

The following are the hypotheses that will be tested during the course of achieving the above goals:

(1) It is hypothesized that the site was occupied twice, once between 1750 - 1800 (most likely 1775-1800) and once between 1820 - 1830. Test implications: There should be a distinct difference between the chronological indicators (such as ceramics) from the two occupations.

(2) Ethnographic accounts from the 1830's and 1840's refer to benched houses. The houses excavated by Smith were unbenched. Of the five houses excavated within the park boundary by Witty, three were unbenched and two were benched. Benched houses may represent the later occupation. Test implications: There should be a distinct difference between the chronological indicators of the benched and unbenched houses.

(3) Krause (1972:114) has suggested that when the trade relationship between a native group and Euro-Americans assumes great importance to the aboriginals' material well being, the native group will tend to locate itself where it is most accessible to traders. It is hypothesized that the occupation of the Kansas Monument site reflects an attempt to be more accessible to Euro-American traders. Test implications: Trade goods from the occupation should reflect a greater variety and abundance than the goods at sites occupied at similar times by the Republican band elsewhere.

(4) Since the Kansas Monument site is one of the southernmost sites known in the Lower Loup - Pawnee continuum, it is hypothesized that the Republicans were dealing with French traders operating out of Saint Louis. Test implications: The Kansas Monument site should show a greater resemblance to sites south of its position, particularly Oklahoma and Texas, rather than north. Regardless of geographical position, this site should show more similarities with the goods from sites in contact with the French rather than the English or other power. Consideration must, of course, be given to whether the situation may be that of a trader drawing on the world market for goods.

It is important to note which power a native group was in contact with since the approaches of the various Euro-American governments to New World populations varied. For example, the Spanish, whose Plains adventure failed, were interested in conquering and Christianizing the natives. The British and the French, on the other hand, were interested only in immediate exploitation of native groups for profit (Holder 1970:7; Secoy 1953:3). Therefore, the changes within native cultures in contact with the British or French would be slower than those in contact with the Spanish.

AN IMPORTANT CONSIDERATION

The overriding concern of this study is with historical archaeology as an anthropological science. In particular, the focus is on historical archaeology on the Great Plains. It is this concern that transcends all other themes in this thesis and permeates the paper throughout. As a discipline, historical archaeology is still at the point where its practitioners must explain their orientations and theoretical foundations. Therefore, before the goals of this study can be met, before the hypotheses can be tested, it is necessary that the reader have an understanding of the author's views and theoretical orientation in historical archaeology. The next chapter will provide an overview of these matters.

2

HISTORICAL ARCHAEOLOGY - SOME
THEORETICAL CONSIDERATIONS

DEFINITION AND DEFENSE OF HISTORICAL ARCHAEOLOGY

It is hoped that this study will stimulate a renewal of interest in historical archaeology on the Plains. Some, however, may disagree with the stated objective on the basis of whether or not work on the Kansas Monument site constitutes historical archaeology. Schuyler (1970:84) defined "historical archaeology" as, "the study of the remains from any historical period." 'Historic sites archaeology' was defined as, "the study of the material manifestation of European culture into the non-European world starting in the 15th Century and ending with industrialization or the present, depending on local conditions." These definitions, which were culled from many different ones in print, would place the archaeology of the Kansas Monument site in the latter category. The differentiation between the two definitions is the result of drawing lines along a chronological continuum. Methods and techniques of analysis are the same in both cases. The epistemology is also the same. It is the contention of the writer that the above definitions constitute hairsplitting. For the purposes of this paper, historical archaeology is defined as *that part of anthropology concerned with the impact of Euro-American cultures on the indigenous cultures of North America and the growth of Euro-American cultures on the continent*. This proposed definition takes as its precedent Schuyler's (1970:83) statement that the term historical archaeology will probably come to overshadow all the other terms that are currently being used.

The above definition expresses, from a North Americanist's standpoint, the same idea as that proposed by Schuyler. It, however, expands upon Wedel's (1938:2) definition of Historic Pawnee archaeology, "the antiquities from documented village sites where the Pawnee are known to have been living in or after circa 1800."

The proposed definition agrees with the others in that it provides for a study of material recovered from sites occupied during the historic period. There is, however, a marked difference between the definition proposed herein and the others. The two definitions cited above stress the study of the physical artifacts alone. The proposed definition calls for the investigation of culture change and process as inferred from the archaeological remains - not an examination of the artifacts alone, but also of the behavioral system that produced them, how they were utilized in that system, and what changes they may have brought about. The words "impact" and "growth" make a great deal of difference. These words are general enough to allow many different aspects of the problem to be explored, but at the same time they clearly suggest that the object is to get beyond the mere study of artifacts.

To define historical archaeology is not to separate it from the remainder of the science. Archaeology should be a unified-integrated field of pursuit, characterized by a particular method of investigation that serves to distinguish it from the other subfields of anthropology. Above all, archaeology is and must remain a part of anthropology. Thus, *a priori*, archaeology and, therefore, historical archaeology have as their ultimate goal the advancement of knowledge about man through their own particularized methods and data. The definition of historical archaeology offered herein is not to suggest that it is a separate entity or field of pursuit, but rather to indicate an emphasis on a particular type of data for the advancement of knowledge.

At this particular time, as at no other and as in probably no other subfield of anthropology, it is necessary that a person who calls himself an historical archaeologist and refers to the work that he does as historical archaeology, define what he means in using these terms. That this is a necessity is the result of the theoretical "upheaval," the "paradigm loss" that is currently plaguing archaeology as a whole, coupled with the internal paradigmatic argument among historical archaeologists.

Leone (1972:26) put forth a personal view on the state of archaeology. He feels that archaeology faces a paradigm crisis because two of the three underlying goals of the science have been exhausted: (1) the outline of the world's prehistory is almost complete and so, "offers little in the way of challenge today"; (2) the reconstruction of past lifeways, for even the most technologically-advanced archaeologist, must be considered a scientific impossibility. The acceptance of these two goals as almost "exhausted," is not universal. This does, however, point out the fact that most archaeological research has focused on these particular problems. The third aim or goal, "cultural analogues to theories such as natural selection," has been attempted only slightly and thus holds promise for the future. Leone then goes on to suggest that "historic" archaeology along with ethno-archaeology and the science of material culture by their "very radical interpretations of what archaeology is all about" may provide archaeologists with the data that are necessary to pursue the one remaining goal.

Historical materials provide fuller sources of data over lengthy periods of time. The historic record can provide details concerning the use of implements, their production, methods of distribution, and the role they played in everyday life. All these data are directly applicable as supplemental information to the archaeological record. It is precisely this sort of information that can be of the most value in assessing the role of material culture in behavioral change. Thus, historical archaeology is extending the horizon of the field by providing data whereby archaeologists in general can address themselves to the problems and study of material culture and human behavior.

Archaeologists have been forced to develop their own analogues to material culture through direct observation, experimentation and replication because most modern ethnographers have neglected this area. It becomes apparent in Leone's (1972:26-7) terms that archaeologists, without being aware of it, have created and are filling a special niche in the study of human behavior. Little is known about the "effects of technology and material culture on other cultural subsystems and vice versa" (Leone 1972:26-7). Yet, it is just such a field of study for which the archaeologist with the techniques, methods, and theory developed during the outlining of World prehistory is suited.

It is precisely to the above study that the proposed definition applies. Historical archaeology in this paper is focused on an interpretation of material culture. Historical archaeology offers unequaled opportunities to investigate material culture, the interaction between different peoples as reflected by their material cultures, and culture change as inferred from material remains. The historic record offers the only existing opportunity to detail a culture change, and then go into the actual archaeological record of the culture that was affected and examine how that change is reflected in material remains.

Hypotheses developed in historical archaeology have the historical record for an experimental control. Utilizing techniques developed by prehistoric archaeologists, an interpretation can be offered for data recovered from historical sites. This interpretation can then be compared with the historical record to see if there is any substance to the included ideas. If there are no serious contradictions between the documentary data and the interpretations based on archaeological data, then it can be accepted that the explanation is valid. Such a model can then be tested for its usefulness in interpreting historical sites for which there are no records and also for its relevance to prehistoric problems.

In saying that the historic record or ethnographic account can be used for experimental control, it must be emphasized that the documentary data are *aids* to producing or substantiating an *archaeologically developed* model. If the archaeologist is totally dependent upon the written record for making interpretations from his archaeologically derived data, then that researcher is bastardizing the archaeological profession. He should use documentary data, but the foundation of his interpretation should be archaeological when his historical-temporal, historical-social, historical-status, historical-function explanations emerge from the archaeological process. There should be a direct and positive nexus between the archaeology and the documents in interpreting the cultural process represented by the patterning seen in the archaeological record. If there is not this connection, then we are frosting history or writing fiction as a veneer over the data with which we began (South 1977:312).

The distinction between documentary data as experimental control and documentary data as explanation is necessary. It is the ability to be able to compare the archaeologically formulated model against the written record that gives historical archaeology its greatest strength. Allowing the written record to function as explanation, meaning using the archaeological data as illustration or to verify the record, is its most dangerous shortcoming. Without the documentary control, historical archaeology would have a methodology no different from prehistoric archaeology. A misuse of this information and historical archaeology becomes no more than a means of padding an historical chronicle.

In distinguishing between the use and abuse of the historical record as outlined above, it is necessary to consider another function of documentation and that is in its role of guide. This function has been previously noted, but must be examined in detail to denote its acceptability as a proper role for documentary data. Historical or ethnographic accounts function as guides when these data tell an archaeologist that at the carefully documented site, A, the introduction of element, R, led to change, Y. This information allows the archaeologist to enter the field knowing that there was a specific behavioral change at the site he is investigating. He can then structure the investigation to maximize retrieval of relevant data. Retrieval is thus directly structured by the problem defined by the documentary data, but the explanation of the archaeologically derived material and the development of a model are not. The latter two activities are carried out in the same manner regardless of whether a site is prehistoric or historic.

Once the archaeologist has completed these activities, he then can return to the written record for substantiation. If in this manner the documentary data verify the model, they can be examined for inferences about non-documented, concurrent cultural changes and/or can be utilized in the formulation of hypotheses about prehistoric or non-recorded historic sites.

HISTORICAL ARCHAEOLOGY AND ITS RELATIONSHIP TO HISTORY AND ETHNOHISTORY

Historical archaeology by its very nature has a close relationship to history and ethnohistory. By definition, historical archaeology would lose its unique character without these two fields. The three also share a relationship in that each is undergoing a change in the paradigms under which it operates. There is no excluding factor that precludes or prevents history, ethnohistory, or historical archaeology from being legitimate fields of scientific inquiry. It is a movement away from particularistic beginnings, towards nomothetic stances that many workers in these fields share.

When considering history or ethnohistory, it is easy to overlook the strides that have been made within these fields. Mildred Wedel (1976:2) has pointed out that ethnohistory is more than just a means of moving from the known to the unknown. Ethnohistorians can, and many do, apply themselves to the study of cultural processes. In fact, a recently proposed definition for ethnohistory describes it as being a division of ethnology that uses historiographical methods as the basis for the formulation of general laws of culture change (M. Wedel 1976:6).

Just as ethnohistory has moved towards the nomothetic approach, so too has history, albeit in a slower and less widespread fashion. This progress is particularly evident in the fields of social history and the "new economic history" or cliometrics. The tardiness of history's movement in comparison with ethnohistory may be due to the fact that ethnohistory is a part of anthropology, which from its earliest beginnings espoused the goals of science. History, on the other hand, until recently had no pretentions to science. The introduction of the scientific method, in this case the use of the hypothetico-deductive model, has had a tremendous impact on the study of economic history in particular and has caused a great deal of rethinking of the subject. It has also met a great deal of resistance (Fogel and Engerman 1974:7). The resistance of the "old school" historians to the "mathematical craze," referring to the use of mathematics and statistics in the popular hypothetico-deductive model, is similar to that of the traditional humanities-oriented historical archaeologist resistance to anthropologically-oriented historical archaeology: in both instances it is a resistance to change from a passive (chronicle) paradigm to an active (scientific) paradigm.

The above paragraphs are intended to show that there are concurrent changes taking place in fields that are concerned with essentially the same subject matter, the historic time period in North America. Again, this is from the North Americanist's viewpoint. All three of the aforementioned fields can be and are used in other parts of the world.

It is in no way suggested that historical archaeology is a part of either history or ethnohistory. There is a dichotomy between the approaches of historical archaeology and the other fields that precludes any sort of relationship beyond interest in common problems or sharing of information. The polarizing factor is that the written record limits history and ethnohistory. Neither an historian nor an ethnohistorian could say much about an historical site of which there is no record. It is, however, the historical archaeologist's function to deal with such sites. Of workers in the various fields that have been discussed, only the historical archaeologist can properly deal with data of unknown historical association. It should also be noted that it is only the historical archaeologist with anthropological training who can deal with such sites most effectively. See South (1977:10-3) for an example of such a situation. The historical archaeologist combines his knowledge of history and ethnography with his archaeological skills, techniques, and knowledge to work with both documented and undocumented archaeological sites. It is this ability to draw on different resources and to manipulate data that the others cannot that truly distinguishes the historical archaeologist from the others.

The three fields mentioned in this section are in the process of changing from chronicle to science. Those who are leading the change share some common attributes: the scientific method and certain data sets, and they can also share a common goal, understanding culture process. Particularly in the case of cliometrics is this so. In a famous cliometric study, *Time on the Cross* (Fogel and Engerman 1974), an anthropologist can appreciate the opportunity to examine cultural behavior associated with slavery and an archaeologist can envision means of answering some of the questions that the authors indicated were impossible. Just such a study is Otto's (1977) "Artifacts and Status Differences - A Comparison of Ceramics from Planter, Overseer, and Slave sites on an Antebellum Plantation." Yet, the authors of *Time on the Cross* were only looking at the economics of slavery, which was their interest. They were apparently not cognizant of the anthropological aspects of their study. Nor, apparently, were they aware of the information that archaeology and anthropology can provide. This only goes to show that the potential for the study of culture process is there but it is often not fulfilled.

Historical archaeologists stand apart from the others in that they use the written record as a tool, not *the* tool. The ultimate source for knowledge in historical archaeology is gleaned from the ground. History does not use an archaeological approach. Historians cannot interpret archaeological data per se. These are important distinctions because they mean that history and ethnohistory will always be limited by the extent of the written record, but that historical archaeology is not.

HISTORICAL ARCHAEOLOGY IN THE ACTIVE VOICE; ANTHROPOLOGY OR THE HUMANITIES

Historical archaeology is a part of anthropological archaeology. This is a point that cannot be stressed enough. It is also a point of much contention. Some of the major workers in the field, and not a few of the younger ones, the "young fogeys" (Flannery 1973:49), are as vociferous in their opposition to a change in the approach of historical archaeology as any of the opponents are to cliometrics or other fields previously mentioned (South 1977:1-28). The dissension within the field is such that Stanley South was led to produce *Method and Theory in Historical Archaeology*, the foremost statement on historical archaeology currently available. This book, the first major work of its kind, should be a turning point for historical archaeology.

South (1977:8) characterizes the traditional historical archaeologist as "particularistic" - interested in individualistic analysis. The particularist is working under the old humanities' paradigm of history as chronicle only. Historical archaeology functions only to add to the chronicle or to aid in verifying it. It is this paradigm that makes it imperative that historical archaeology not be relegated to the humanities. It has already been noted that such a use of historical archaeology constitutes "bastardizing" the profession. What has not been pointed out is that data recovered by workers operating under the humanities paradigm are usually unsuitable for future use by a researcher with nomothetic interests. Thus, historical archaeologists who operate under the humanities paradigm are not only not living up to the obligations of archaeology as a science, they are also destroying information that could be of use in developing general laws of culture process.

Considering the changes that have taken place within the field of history during the past 20 years, one may tend to think of the particularists in historical archaeology as being voices from the past. Yet, an analysis of the content of articles appearing during the past 15 years in *The Conference on Historic Site Archaeology Papers* and the Society for Historical Archaeology journal, *Historical Archaeology*, the major outlets for historical archaeologists, reveals that 86% of the works are particularistic in orientation (South 1977: 17, 22)! It is an unavoidable fact that the historical archaeologist with nomothetic interests is in a distinct minority. In archaeology as a whole, the balance between the "new" and the "old," between nomothetic studies and particularism, is decidedly in the favor of the former. With historical archaeology, the contest is just beginning. Not only is the particularist alive and well, he is also publishing.

One of the best known of the particularists is Ivor Noel Hume, chief archaeologist for the Colonial Williamsburg restoration project and a prolific author on particularistic problems (Noel Hume 1969, 1970, 1974 and many articles). In one of his best-known works he stated that (Noel Hume 1969: 14-5),

> *In our anxiety to wrest archaeology away from the pot-hunters and dilettante collectors, we tend to overcompensate by elevating it to the ranks of the sciences. In truth it has no business there; its place is with the arts.*

Similar views can be found in many statements on methods and principles in historical archaeology (e.g. Walker 1967:23-34; Dollar 1968:2-30). And these are not aberrant holdovers from another time. These people, until workers such as Stanley South came to prominence, were the dominant voices of historical archaeology. There are still many who follow these beliefs. Just as Leone (1972:17) suggests that archaeology finds the answers to problems one paradigm old, in relation to the rest of anthropology, many historical archaeologists are operating under paradigms one or two behind the rest of archaeology. With this the case, it is imperative that the historical archaeologist state his position. In final remarks on the nature of historical archaeology and its relationship to other fields, I will say that in working with the Kansas Monument site I am engaging in the study of historical archaeology. I have in no way absented myself from anthropological archaeology by so doing. Rather, I am in fact helping to broaden the database for anthropological archaeology as a science of material culture and human behavior. By calling myself an historical archaeologist I have only delimited a field of interest. It is similar to saying that one is a Plains or Southeastern archaeologist. The only difference being that instead of geographical boundaries, the limits of historical archaeology are temporal.

HISTORICAL ARCHAEOLOGY AND ITS RELATIONSHIP TO PREHISTORIC ARCHAEOLOGY

The historical archaeologist often finds, among his colleagues, who are engaged in other forms of archaeology, a rather poor conception of what historical archaeology is. This limited view of historical archaeology reflects the volume of particularistic publications: Historical archaeology presents a particularistic face and so becomes associated with the particularistic point of view (South 1977: xiii-xiv). The anthropological historical archaeologist must be concerned with his colleagues' views of the field. It has been the author's previous experience that too many prehistoric archaeologists have an attitude that can be characterized, as a pound of potsherds is better than a ton of historical record. There is actually not much sense in that last statement and the same is true for the bias against historical archaeology. The ongoing processes of behavioral change are not altered nor do they cease to exist simply because of the advent of written records, regardless of whether or not those records come from within or without the culture. The complexities of these changes may increase but the underlying relationships remain the same.

One of the complaints of anthropological historical archaeologists is that the average anthropological archaeologist who digs an historic site often lacks an appreciation for the importance of the historic record (Fontana 1965:64). This has also been one of the humanities-oriented historical archaeologists' major criticisms directed towards anthropological archaeologists (Noel Hume 1969:12-3; Walker 1967:24-7). Thus the traditional anthropological archaeologist is guilty of not utilizing the historical record as it should be used, and the traditional historical archaeologist is guilty of not progressing beyond it. With the rise of the historical archaeologist as an anthropological archaeologist, the combined knowledge, theories, resources, techniques, and so forth of both the historian and the anthropologist are directed at the problems of historical archaeology (South 1977:12).

There have been studies or reports involving historic sites from virtually the earliest days of archaeology. Any archaeologist excavating a site with a post-contact component is forced to deal with historic materials. It is the manner in which the historic components of a site are dealt with that is of concern. In the instance of an Indian site that falls within the historic period—on the Plains this could include the Historic period and protohistoric period as well—anthropological archaeologists tend to concentrate on the aboriginal materials and give the Euro-American artifacts little attention. Krause (1972) does this, but is above average in that he does not overlook the historic goods completely. Lehmer (1971) treats historic materials in a somewhat better but still unsatisfactory manner. The best treatment that the historic trade goods receive in such reports is a description and this is sometimes reduced to the simplest of terms such as, "European," "American," "Euro-American," or "Spanish." Interpretations or explanations based on such sites often take only the aboriginal material into consideration (Fontana 1965:64). The "European goods" aspect of the site, which in some instances may exceed over half of the total artifact inventory, may find mention as evidence of trade or white contact. This is an unfortunate misuse of the archaeological record.

In the available literature one can find journal articles and books devoted to early trade and trade goods (e.g. Hanson 1956; Russell 1962, 1967; Woodward 1946, 1970) on the Plains and throughout the country. Yet, none of these deal with the archaeological perspective of these goods. Each uses archaeological data to supplement and/or illustrate the written record. This state of affairs reflects Smith's comment concerning the response to his call (Smith 1950a) for archaeologists to publish their data on trade goods; "There was no response. There was no one doing work with trade goods on the Plains" (Smith personal communication). He was not referring to a complete lack of interest but to the lack of interest displayed by archaeologists. Those workers with historic material on their sites were not asking questions such as, "What do these items mean?" Nor was there much interest in the answers found by those who did ask.

The prehistorians who neglected the historic trade goods that occurred in sites were overlooking the significance of such artifacts. The post-contact period represents the meeting of two or more cultures, aboriginal and Euro-American. Trade goods are among the best inferential tools archaeologists have for understanding the changes that resulted from the meeting. Both the prehistoric and historical archaeologists should be interested in culture process and, therefore, culture change, i.e., behavior change. Trade goods, if nothing else, represent change - a change that occurred slowly at first but resulted in "hardly any resemblance between what had been and what was" (Quimby 1966:43-4).

Why such obvious indicators of material culture change as trade goods were ignored is a reflection of the anthropological archaeologists' bias and this bias is more a reflection of ignorance than any other single cause. This is not ignorance in the sense of stupidity, but rather in the sense of a lack of appreciation for something potentially valuable. Some of the criticisms leveled at anthropological "scientific" archaeology by the traditional historical archaeologists often show the latter to be confusing the methods of science with the techniques (e.g. Walker 1967:26-7). The anthropological archaeologist may be guilty of essentially the same thing in ignoring historical material. Approaching artifacts without a battery of edge angle, platform width, sherd thickness, and the other measures that are commonly employed in describing prehistoric artifacts, may tend to leave the anthropological "scientific" archaeologist feeling stripped of his "science" and to be called unscientific is the anathema of the modern archaeologist. However, as Leslie White (1938) so aptly put it, "Science is sciencing." The aforementioned attributes are not applicable to most historic goods though some workers have used them. There are, however, other criteria and measures that can be used to conduct an attribute level analysis of historic materials, the point being that it is not the material being dealt with and the techniques being used that determine whether one is being scientific or not, but the ideas and methods behind the data manipulation. The scientific method is just as applicable to historic sites and goods as it is to prehistoric ones and possibly it is even more effectively used with the former than the latter since the historical record can act as an experimental control.

As an example of the sort of potentially useful types of information historical archaeology can produce is Krause's (1972) "The Leavenworth Site: Archaeology of an Historic Arikara Community." This monograph suffers from some of the shortcomings of an historic site report published by an anthropological archaeologist who is not primarily an historical archaeologist. The emphasis is on the aboriginal artifacts and the historic trade material is treated primarily by description. Yet, Krause did not ignore the trade goods question and as a result the hypotheses presented during the development of his model are quite exciting. It is not necessary to detail all the hypotheses here; one will be sufficient to show what the prehistorian can gain from historical archaeology. One of Krause's (1972:114) hypotheses is that as Euro-American trade goods become more important to a native group, that group will tend to locate itself in areas where it is more easily accessible to traders. If this hypothesis holds true after testing, the implications for prehistoric archaeology become obvious. Movements of prehistoric peoples may have strong links with trade. What aspects of trade were important enough to merit a move closer to a trade source? Could seasonally occupied sites that are reoccupied over a long period of time also have a trade as well as a subsistence function?

The above questions can be answered through historical archaeology. Such considerations are indicative of the problems faced by all archaeologists. It is in the best interest of archaeological science that anthropological historical archaeology be nurtured and encouraged. Only historical archaeologists, with the aid of incontestable historic data, have the opportunity to test some of the basic assumptions of archaeology. Consider Deetz and Dethlefsen's (1965) study on seriation using gravestones in New England, for example. Using written records and archaeological evidence, historical archaeologists are far better equipped to isolate and understand human behavior than pre-historians. In this sense, the historical archaeologist has the archaeological record, which is undeniable evidence of what was done, and the written record, which is a statement by the makers of the archaeological record of what they thought they were doing. The result of having both sources approaches that unique state of knowledge called understanding. This is living up to archaeology's goal as a science. This is helping archaeologists as students of behavior and material culture's influences on behavior, to better understand some of the processes involved.

19

3

1949 EXCAVATIONS AT THE KANSAS MONUMENT SITE

The 1949 excavations centered on exposing the remains of two earth lodges (Features 3 and 4), exploring two bell-shaped cache pits (Features 1 and 11), and testing the fortification wall (Feature 2) within the fenced-in area. In addition, a test trench was excavated through a house (Feature 12) in the plowed field to the south. The following is a complete listing of the features designated by Smith during the course of the excavations:

F. 1 Bell-shaped cache pit west of the granite monument

F. 2 - Fortification wall encircling the site

F. 3 - House #1

F. 4 - Leaner trench on the interior of House #1

F. 5 - Buffalo skull inside House #1

F. 6 - House #2

F. 7 - Borrow pit

F. 8 - Thatch from House #2

F. 9 - Surface cache on the floor of House #2

F. 10 - Charred remains of a twined mat

F. 11 - Bell-shaped cache pit

F. 12 - Test trench in house circle in south field

HOUSES

Excavation of a house was begun by extending a trench, five feet wide from outside wall to outside wall, through the center of the house. This procedure resulted in exposing the central fireplace and floor of the house. The remainder of the house was excavated by working radially out from the central fireplace, following the contour of the floor. There were no grid units within the houses. As postmolds were encountered they were cored and measured, but were not profiled. All measurements were taken in the English system.

To avoid compounding the rounding error by using a metric conversion, the original measurements have been retained.

House 1

Surface Indications: A pronounced pit with a raised rim, approximately 45 feet in diameter. (Figure 3)

Figure 3. House 1.

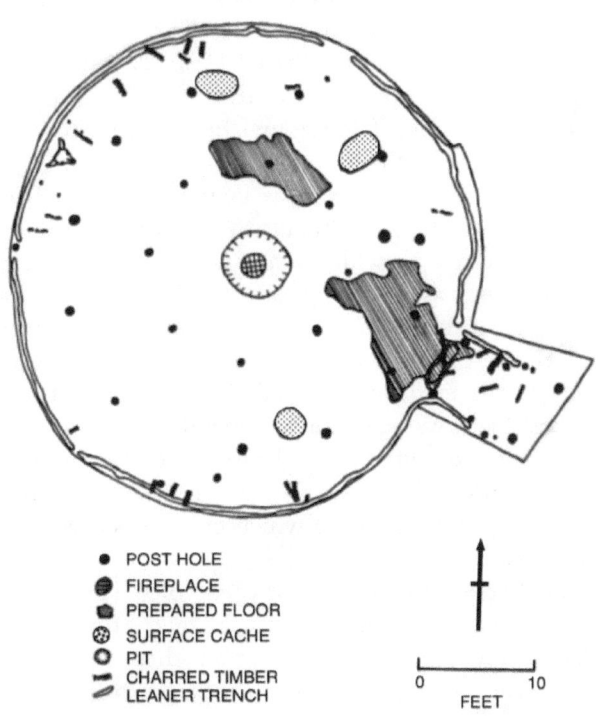

- ● POST HOLE
- ◉ FIREPLACE
- ◉ PREPARED FLOOR
- ⊛ SURFACE CACHE
- ○ PIT
- ▬ CHARRED TIMBER
- ⬤ LEANER TRENCH

0   10
FEET

Form: Roughly circular with a mean diameter of 39.5 feet.

Entrance: Oriented to the southeast. Length, 10 feet; width, 6 feet. Marked by two parallel rows of five vertical posts each. The posts varied from 4 to 9 inches in diameter and 4 to 19 inches in depth. Parallel leaner trenches of 4 and 6 feet were present. There was a 4-foot long sill in the entrance. It had been covered with a patch of prepared flooring that had been burned orange in color.

Floor: Basin shaped, sloping inward to the center where the central fireplace was located in a pit. Two sections of prepared flooring were preserved. The smallest extant section had dimensions of 10.5 feet in length and 4.5 feet in width. This section was along the north side and had been burned black. The larger section was at the entrance of the lodge and covered the sill. This patch of prepared flooring was burned orange and had maximum dimensions of 10 feet in length and 5.5 feet in width. A fragment of burned flooring recovered from the bottom of one of the postmolds suggests that the floor was prepared and burned prior to the placement of the posts.

Post Holes: Eight center posts spaced approximately 6 feet 3 inches from each other on a radius of approximately 8.75 feet from the center of the house. Eleven outer posts were spaced at 5 to 9 foot intervals at a distance of 15 to 16.5 feet from the center. These posts ranged from 7 to 11 inches in diameter and had depths of 11 to 29 inches. The two outer posts at the entrance were only 4 feet apart.

Roof: Charred remains of horizontal beams were found radiating out from the center on the floor.

Fireplaces: This house had only a central fireplace. Root action had disturbed the hearth making it difficult to discern. It had a diameter of 2 feet. It was located in a pit with a diameter of 5.75 feet. No evidence of the prepared flooring was present around the fireplace. In and around this fireplace were metal arrow points and the remains of their production, chert flakes, one rim sherd, and one body sherd. It is significant that this fireplace contains the evidence for both lithic and metal tool production. This fact implies that it was necessary to maintain the production of certain lithic tools for which a suitable metal replacement could not be obtained through trade or produced by the Pawnee themselves. There is too little evidence to allow speculation as to which chipped stone tools remained in production the longest.

Cache Pits: There were no interior cache pits. Three surface caches of charred corn were discovered. These ranged from 2.5 to 4 feet in maximum diameter and had a thickness of 3 inches.

Other Features: Bison skull shrine, situated on the axis that passes through the central fireplace and bisects the entrance. The shrine was on a wooden altar evidenced by the remains of the four corner posts and one of the horizontal beams. These altars usually were made of clay (Wedel 1936:43-51). The 1966 excavation by Witty revealed a similar altar in House 6 (Witty 1968:3). A leaner trench varying from 1 to 6 inches in depth and 3 to 6 inches in width was discernible along most of the lodge circle perimeter. It was not visible at the entrance.

Artifacts: See Table 1.

Table 1. Artifact Distribution by Excavation Unit

Artifact	House 1	House 2	Feature 1	Feature 2	Feature 7	Burial 1
POTTERY						
Rim Sherds	12	14		1	15	
Body Sherds	30	42		1	3	
SCRAPERS						
Hafted	1	1				
Expanding	2	2				
Elliptical	1	8				
Discoidal	3	2				
BIFACE	1					
GUNFLINTS						
Aboriginal	3	2				
European	2					
HAMMERSTONES						
Cobble	2	2				
Discoidal	2					
PECKING STONES						
GROVED MAULS	2					
STONE BALLS		1				
METATE			1			
MANO		1				
MORTAR	1					
GRINDING PALLETTES						
Amorphous	1			1		
Ovoid		2				
SHAFT SMOOTHER	1	16		2		
ABRADERS	4	4				
WHETSTONES	3	1				
PIPES						
Elbow		2				
Preform	1	1				
Fragment	1	1				
PETRIFIED WOOD	1					
HEMATITE	X	X				
MISCELLANEOUS GROUND STONE	3	2				
UTILIZED FLAKES AND CHIPS	X	X				
GROUND STONE FRAGMENTS	1	12				
ROUGH STONE		1				
SCAPULA HOES	1		7			
BONEFLESHER					1	
SHAFT WRENCH	1					
ELK HORN SCRAPER	1	2				
WOODEN MORTAR		1				
IRON HOES						
Hoop Skirt		1				
Pear		1				
Round		1				
IRON KNIVES	4	1				
IRON AXES	1	2				
GUN PARTS	10	7			1	
METAL PROJECTILE POINTS	7	4				
KETTLE PARTS	2	1				
Fragments	X	X				
AWLS	2					
NAILS		1	1			
LEAD RING		1				
COPPER TINKLER	1	1				
IRON BRACELET						1
BUCKLE	1					
IRON SCRAPER						
MISCELLANEOUS METAL	X	X				
BOTTLE	1					
GLASS BEADS	1	274				198
MATTING		1				

House 2

Surface Indications: Visible pit, no further information was recorded.

Form: Roughly circular with a mean diameter of 34 feet. Smith (personal communication) feels that the outer limits of the house may not have been reached. Therefore, the mean diameter may have been greater.

Entrance: Oriented to the southeast. Indicated by the presence of parallel leaner trenches connecting end posts. Estimated length, 8 feet; width, 6 feet. Post molds in the leaner trenches varied from 2.5 to 3 inches in diameter and 1.5 to 3.5 inches in depth. End posts varied from 7.5 inches to 10.5 inches in diameter and 12 to 20 inches in depth. A 4-foot long sill was also present (Figure 4).

Figure 4. House 2.

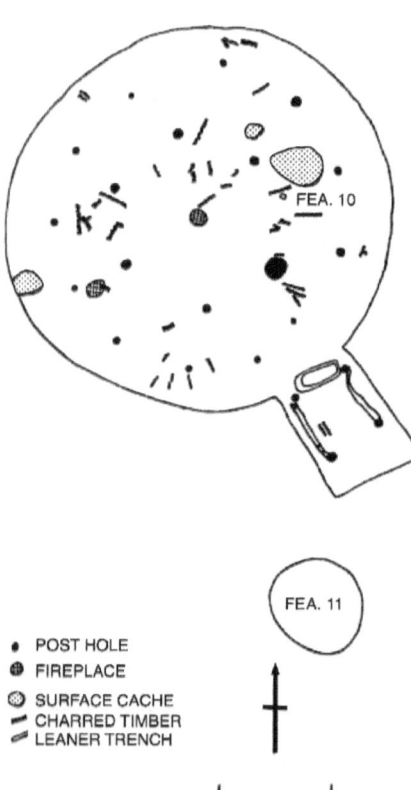

- POST HOLE
- FIREPLACE
- SURFACE CACHE
- CHARRED TIMBER
- LEANER TRENCH

FEA. 11

0   FEET   10

Floor: Basin shaped, sloping inward to the central fireplace. There was no evidence of prepared flooring.

Post Holes: Six center posts ranging from 8.5 to 22.5 inches in diameter and 11.5 to 24 inches in depth were spaced between 6 and 9 feet from each other on a radius 7.5 to 8 feet from the central fireplace. Twelve outer posts were spaced at intervals of 5 to 8.5 feet from each other within 12 to 13.5 feet from the central fireplace. These posts varied from 5 to 11 inches in diameter and their depths had a range of 11 to 22 inches.

Roof: Charred remains of horizontal beams were found radiating out from the center of the lodge. A small portion of roof thatch was also uncovered. The thatch has been tentatively identified as cottonwood.

Fireplaces: One main fireplace in the center and one secondary fireplace in the southwest portion of the lodge, almost directly between a center post and an outer post. The central fireplace had a diameter of 1.5 feet. The secondary fireplace was oblong with a maximum length of 2 feet and width of 1.5 feet. Multiple fireplaces are not unusual in Pawnee lodges. The occurrence of more than one fireplace may be related to the number of families inhabiting the lodge.

Cache Pits: No interior cache pits. Three surface caches of charred corn were present. These ranged from 1.5 to 4.5 feet in diameter. No measure of thickness was recorded. The cache in the southwestern part of the house was in association with an iron hoe, an antler tine, a mussel shell and some yellow pigment. This may be a cache of seed corn. The hoe would have been for cultivation, the tine probably for punching holes during planting.

Other Features: Four "caches" of red and yellow pigment (ground hematite) were present near the largest surface cache of charred corn.

Artifacts: See Table 1.

Feature 12

Feature 12 was a house in the south field that was tested. Very little was recorded about the results of the test. Based on the field map, the structure was approximately 33 feet in diameter. The test trench was approximately 42 feet long and 5 feet wide. The floor of the house was approximately 12 inches below the surface. Some evidence of prepared flooring was recovered. There is no record of any artifacts recovered from this house. This is the total amount of data available for Feature 12.

Discussion

A comparison between the two houses that were completely excavated revealed incontestable differences in construction. By any scale of measure, House 1 was constructed in a manner superior to that of House 2. The discovery by Witty (1968:3) of one virtually identical (House 6) and one almost identical structure (House 5) cannot be dismissed as coincidental.

There is obviously a pattern of building behavior involved. Neither Strong (1935) nor Wedel (1936) reported anything similar. There was apparently something special associated with these houses. The distinguishing characteristics were buffalo shrines on wooden platforms, not present in House 5, the museum, excavated by Witty, fired clay floors, and eight center posts. It has been held by most authorities that the number of posts in a house is not a significant detail. From the material that was recovered, it can be said that House 1 was not a ceremonial structure, per se, but may have been the residence of an important person. Without further data, however, this is pure speculation. All that can be said is that House 1 and similar structures were built with great care. They were purposefully built to conform to a set pattern. Given further information, these houses may become important to the understanding of the structure and changes in Pawnee culture.

ADDITIONAL EXCAVATIONS

FORTIFICATION WALL

The fortification wall, Feature 2 (Figure 2), which originally encircled most of the village, was probed with five test trenches placed at different points along its length. There are few data available on the results of the tests

Since the data are so limited, it is not necessary to examine each test unit. Rather, the data from each of the tests will be consolidated allowing a reconstruction of the probable appearance of the wall to be made.

The wall was built by piling up dirt from nearby exterior borrow pits. Posts were placed so that they extended at an angle from the apex of the wall, thus forming out-slanting pickets. There was no indication of vertically placed posts. It appears to have been common practice to throw refuse over the wall, particularly at those sections which bordered the borrow pits. During testing it was possible to define the limits of the fortification by noting where the limits of midden deposits were. Refuse was also mixed in with the dirt that composed the wall. This may be due to borrow pits being used for midden areas before dirt removal activity was completed. The dirt used to build the wall came from the borrow pits only, as there was no associated ditch or moat.

Grange (1968:152-3) has suggested that fortified villages are late in time, possibly post 1820. Considering the fact that the Republican band was having trouble continuously with the Kansa and Osage while it occupied the Republican River valley, the late date may not be justified. The Hill site, which Grange places at 1775-1810 (Grange 1974: 326), was a fortified village (Wedel 1936:35). Therefore, it is possible for the Kansas Monument site to have an early date. Fortification would seem to be a function of the individual village's situation, rather than a temporal, culture wide phenomenon.

CACHE PITS

Smith excavated two cache pits (Features 1 and 11; Figure 2). These pits, like the others, were plainly visible as small depressions in the earth's surface.

Feature 1: The first cache pit excavated was located west of the granite monument. It was bell-shaped, which was typical of Pawnee cache pits. The pit had a maximum depth of 57 inches and a maximum diameter of 60.5 inches at a depth of 30 inches. Dispersed throughout the levels of the pit were a few kernels of charred corn, some charcoal, and a few sherds. When the bottom of the pit was reached at 57 inches, seven bison scapula hoes were uncovered.

Feature 11. The second cache pit, also bell-shaped, had a mouth diameter of 45 inches, a maximum diameter of 51 inches at 38 inches below the surface, and a depth of 74 inches. It was located south of Feature 6. This pit yielded very little in the way of cultural detritus. There was some charcoal and a few bits of pottery scattered through the pit fill. The bottom of the pit was covered with a mass of animal bones with bison predominating.

Discussion. Considering the fact that both caches contained little cultural material, there is a temptation to attribute this to something that would prevent their having been filled with refuse, as was usually the case once the stored corn had been removed. Sterile caches, however, are not unusual (Wedel 1936:54). The virtual lack of refuse in these pits may reflect the fact that discarding material outside the fortification wall or into a communal trash pit was a preferred behavior. This inference is supported by the quantity of material recovered from the borrow pits and area on the exterior of the wall and the midden deposit, Feature 7. It is also possible that the pits had covers.

BURIALS

Tests for burials were concentrated between the village site and the bluffs. All but one of the tests were negative, one revealed a disturbed burial on a bluff edge 400 yards to the northwest of the monument.

Burial 1: This burial was the only one located by Smith. There is no doubt that it was disturbed, since at the bottom of the pit a .22 caliber bullet and some tinfoil such as that wrapped around chewing gum were found.

The burial pit was 62 inches deep. The mouth of the pit had a diameter of 32 inches and the bottom had a diameter of 27 inches. The maximum diameter of the pit was 39.5 inches that occurred at a depth of 26 inches. These dimensions may not reflect the actual size and shape of the pit since it was disturbed.

The skeletal material was not in its original orientation and so was not recorded in situ. Sufficient parts of the skeletons remained to determine that the burial had contained two occupants: an adult female and a child of unknown sex.

The only artifacts recovered were a collection of trade beads and some red and yellow ochre. There may have been other material, probably removed by the looters.

Typical Pawnee burial procedure was to dig a pit with an undercut and then deposit the body in a flexed or semi-flexed position in the undercut. Grave goods of aboriginal manufacture or trade items were added. Red and yellow ochre were almost invariably included in burials. There is no evidence to suggest that this burial differed from those of the traditional style.

4

ARTIFACTS

The following pages contain a type-by-type description of all the material recovered by Smith's excavations. Only the excavated material is used in order to maintain control of the data. If surface collections and excavated material provided by amateurs were included, the data would be seriously skewed due to mixing. Within these aforementioned collections is material far too late in time to have been part of the Pawnee occupation. Since it is impossible to control the mixing of artifacts from different occupations when using grab surface collections, only excavated material can be used. Smith recovered the bulk of the artifacts described below, but rim sherds recovered by Witty are included. This thesis does not attempt to include all the material recovered by the Kansas State Historical Society's excavations because it is the Society's intention to publish a full report on their work.

The type descriptions are presented in as much detail as possible and all pertinent artifacts are illustrated. This detail is necessary to facilitate the development of chronological and geographical controls for the trade goods and to provide a better understanding of the traditional Pawnee material culture. There is a definite need for an understanding of the temporal and geographical distribution of trade goods. There is an equal need to understand the changes in aboriginal material culture as Euro-American goods became available. Wedel's (1936) work is really no more than an introduction as the title indicates. No one has turned any attention to a more comprehensive investigation of the basic composition and changes within Pawnee material culture.

It is the author's conviction that trade goods can become very powerful tools for dating historic sites. These artifacts can also contribute to an understanding of the changes that were occurring in aboriginal culture. By understanding which goods are entering the system and which are dropping out, the archaeologist is gaining the best picture available to him of the behavioral changes happening in a given culture. Yet, all of these things rest on researchers devoting study to trade goods and other historic artifacts comparable to the work that has been done with prehistoric assemblages. The first step to the understanding of these materials is in sections such as this. Herein are the first faltering steps of understanding.

The most outstanding work on historic goods to date is Stone's (1974) work on the material from Fort Michilimackinac. The present report has followed his guidelines wherever possible. Most of the material presented in this section takes the form of what Stone called informal type descriptions. In some instances Stone's formal classifications were adaptable to the artifacts and can be noted in the text.

Table 2 provides a listing of the sites used for comparison. The comparison of the material from the Kansas Monument site with the assemblages at other sites allows Hypotheses 1 and 4 to be tested (see Chapter I). The implications for the testing of the hypotheses are as follows:

Table 2. List of Comparative Historic Sites.

SITE	DATES	SOURCE
Deer Creek, OK	1735-1760	Sudbury 1976
Fatherland, MS	1682-1729	Neitzel 1965
Fort Michilimackinac, MI	1718-1787	Stone1974 Maxwell & Binford 1961
Gilbert, TX	1750-1775	Jelks 1967
Guebert, IL	1719-1813	Good 1972
Hill, NE	1775-1810	Wedel 1936
Leavenworth, SD	1804-1823	Krause 1972
Linwood, NE	1777-1809 1851-1859	Carlson 1973
Longest, OK	1750-1800	Bell et al. 1967
Pearson, TX	1775-1830	Duffield & Jelks 1961
Plattner, MO	1727-1777	Chapman 1959
Rosebaugh Lake, TX	1719-1778	Miroir et al. 1973
Womack, TX	1700-1730	Harris et al. 1965

If the Kansas Monument site is late in time (1821-1831), then the trade goods from it should resemble the assemblages from sites of the same period. If it is an early site, then the artifacts should resemble those from early sites.

If the Pawnee at this site were dealing with the French, then the goods should be identifiable as French and should resemble the goods from other French contact sites.

If there is a temporal difference between the houses, this should show up in the trade goods, i.e. if the houses were inhabited at the same time, then the goods from each house should be comparable. One house should not show affinity with early sites and the other affinity with late sites. Neither should one show a relationship with French contact sites and the other with non-French contact sites, if they are coeval. This test implication also affects Hypothesis 2.

CERAMIC ARTIFACTS

On the basis of frequency, the ceramic assemblage from the Kansas Monument site can be considered the largest of the aboriginally produced artifact classes. Though the number of individual specimens is high, only four pottery types, two wares without defined types, and a single inclusive category of figurines are represented. This section can be one of the most important in this study. No analysis of the pottery has been undertaken since the publication of Grange's (1968) study on Pawnee and Lower Loup pottery. Considering the impact that study had on the accepted position of the Kansas Monument site in the Historic Pawnee sequence, a typological analysis of the material is necessary. Additionally, the pottery from the site is of the utmost importance in testing the first and second hypotheses put forth in Chapter I. In light of Grange's recent work on formula-dating Historic Pawnee and Lower Loup sites using pottery types, this material becomes even more conducive to testing the aforementioned hypotheses (Grange 1974).

FIGURINES

Figurines are rare on Pawnee sites. A few fragments representing quadrupeds of some sort were recovered from the Hill site (Wedel 1936:70). All the specimens from the Kansas Monument site are fragments. Since there are no complete specimens, it was decided not to divide the fragments into more than one type although there are several distinct morphological varieties present.

Figurine Fragments (Figure 5g). The most complete specimen is an anthropomorphic figurine without arms, broken just below the point where the legs joined the body. Pinching the clay at the narrow end of the piece formed a head. A slash represents the mouth but no other facial features are present. The front of the piece is slightly convex. The back is flat. In its broken condition, the piece is 35mm long, (sic) wide at the shoulders, and 16mm wide at the point where the legs join the body. A maximum thickness of 7mm occurs just above the break. The paste has a very fine-grained sand temper, as do the rest of the fragments. The sand may be a natural paste inclusion rather than a purposefully added tempering agent. This piece, as were the other fragments, was recovered from House 2.

Figure 5. Ceramic Rim Sherds and Figurine: a. Webster Collar Braced; b. & c. Wright Collared Ware; d. Butler Braced; e. & f. Webster Bowl Ware; g. Figurine.

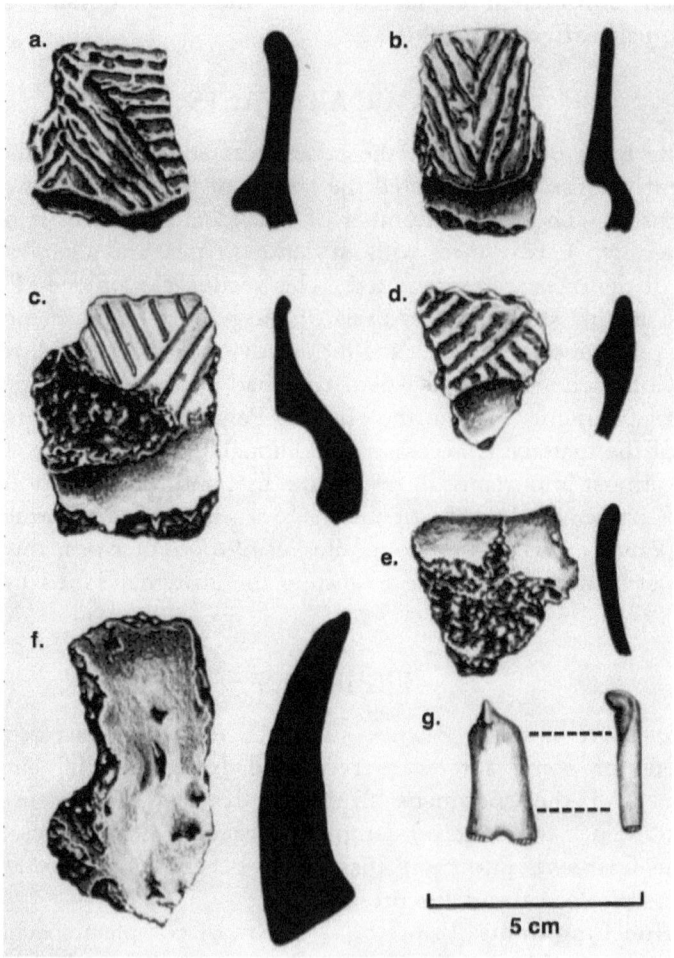

5 cm

Two fragments were recovered from the fireplace of House 2. One specimen is from the upper half of a figurine, the other from the lower half, but the two are not from the same piece. The upper half fragment is ovoid in cross section. It had a pinched head similar to the one above, but the head was on the front of the piece rather than resting on shoulders. Punctates went all the way around the piece on the lateral edges. At its thickest, the piece measured 5mm. The lower half fragment is also ovoid in cross-section. If it were whole, this would have been the largest of the figurines. At the point where the legs joined the body, the fragment is 20mm wide. Just above this point the piece reaches its maximum thickness of 8mm. One of the convex surfaces is covered with incised diagonal lines, upper left to lower right. These lines were made with a pliable tool while the clay was still soft (Shepard 1956:188-9).

The fourth and last fragment from House 2 is in poor condition. Its form suggests the posterior portion of a quadruped (bison?). The advanced deterioration of the specimen precludes any measurements.

Discussion. It may be of importance that figurines were limited to House 2. No ethnographic accounts of the Pawnee record such figurines. They may represent an idiosyncratic behavior on the part of the ceramicist that lived in the house. It should be noted that the only example of a miniature pot in the collection excavated by Smith (specimen number 14129-1) was recovered in association with the quadruped fragment. The significance of the accumulation of these small items is unknown.

POTTERY

The current knowledge about the technology involved in the production of Pawnee pottery is based primarily on the analysis of archaeologically derived samples. Ethnographic accounts (Wedel 1936:62-3) are few. This lack of documentation reflects the declining importance of pottery as Euro-American substitutes became easier to obtain. It is also a reflection of the fact that the years during which most of the ethnographic reports were written and museum collections made, postdated the cessation of pottery making among the Pawnee.

There are only three readily available sources that examine Pawnee ceramics in any detail. These three sources are Strong (1935), Wedel (1936), and Grange (1968). The order of publication for these three sources reflects qualitative and quantitative increases in the knowledge of Pawnee pottery. Grange (1968) now stands as the authoritative text on the subject.

The results of the analysis performed on the ceramic material from the Kansas Monument site do not add any significant information about the technological process involved in Pawnee pottery making. The importance of the analysis is its effect upon the relationship between this site and the other historic Pawnee sites. The effect, which will be discussed later, requires a complete reappraisal of the current state of knowledge about the historic Pawnee period.

CONSTRUCTION OF A PAWNEE POT - THE KANSAS MONUMENT EXAMPLE

The pottery, like most Pawnee pottery, was the product of hand modeling and paddle and anvil shaping or finishing.

After shaping, smoothing the surface of the vessel while it was still wet was common. Several of the Kansas Monument site specimens were scraped with a pliable tool while the pot was leather hard, Shepard (1954:188) provides the criteria used in determining this aspect of the construction process.

A questionable account from an elderly informant of Grinnell, reported pottery was made by molding clay over the rounded end of a tree (Grinnell 1893:255-6). There was no evidence for such a process in the material. Grinnell related in the same account a report by Dunbar that the Pawnee used a willow twig mold to produce pottery. There was no evidence for this process discovered either.

Simple stamping was the most common surface treatment. There is good evidence that floating and polishing, including the combination of simple stamping and polishing, were also practiced. The only interior surface treatment noted was a low incidence of slipping. The interior slip was noted on sherds from several types but was not prevalent. Smoothing over the surface treatment was not common.

The most common form of decoration was incising or trailing designs on the rim. There was variation in the execution of similar designs as can be noted in Figure 5. This variation can probably be attributed to the idiosyncratic behavior of the individual potter, i.e. certain designs were favored by the group, but the way the design was executed was a function of the particular potter's learning and ability. It can be seen in Figure 5 that some designs were executed in broad strokes, some in narrow, some were done while the paste was still rather plastic, and others after the clay had reached a leather hard state. There is also evidence to suggest that designs were occasionally smoothed over.

Decoration was commonly restricted to the rim but there is a limited amount of evidence for decoration on the shoulder and body of certain vessels. This evidence will be discussed under the appropriate type sections later.

Sand and a mixture of sand and calcite were the most common tempering agents present. The calcite is actually aragonite, a mineral with the same chemical composition ($CaCO_3$) as calcite but with a fibrous crystal

34

form (Tolsted and Swineford 1957:39-40). Grange (1968:44) noted that grit temper was the most common among Pawnee and Lower Loup pottery. Since his discussion of grit-tempered paste refers to "crushed granite or sand," the prevalence of sand tempering at the Kansas Monument site cannot be considered contrary to his findings. In the present study, sand was defined as rounded siliceous particles while grit was defined as angular bits of crushed rock. Therefore, these two different tempering agents should not be included under a single name as seems to be the case with Grange's statement.

The potters used three fairly distinct varieties of clay. Two of the varieties account for approximately 90-95% of the sample. The most common clay is very coarse with a laminated structure. It required large amounts of temper, estimated at greater than 50% in many cases. The clay's lamellar structure, probably the function of some form of wedging, may be responsible for the tendency among the sherds to split parallel to the exterior and interior surfaces. Grange noted that the use of similar clays was common in Pawnee and Lower Loup assemblages (Grange 1968:44).

The second most common clay was of a higher quality than that just described. An examination of a fresh break on a sherd made from this clay shows no laminated structure. Instead, the break has a fine granular appearance. There does not seem to be any tendency for the sherds to break saccharoidally. Sherds made from this type of clay are not heavily tempered.

The minority clay has a high sand content. The sand is very fine grained and uniform in size; it probably represents a natural paste inclusion rather than a tempering agent. Large grains of sand, in the size range of the sand grains used as temper in other pastes, are present in sherds made from this type of clay. When these large grains occur, the sherd is considered sand tempered. In these cases, however, the temper is much less than 10%, the sparsest recorded. Without the large sand grains, sherds made from this paste would be considered untempered or they would be placed in a category for naturally tempered pastes. A fresh break on a sherd made from this paste has a fine, granular appearance, much finer than the paste described above. There is no lamellar structure. This paste is almost exclusively associated with Webster Bowl Ware sherds. Grange (1968:45) noted that Webster Bowl Ware sherds tended to be sparsely tempered in comparison to the other sherd types. The data from the Kansas Monument site support this observation, but the significance of it is not yet understood.

Although it was noticed that the one particular variety of clay did tend to be associated with a particular pottery type, there was no similar pattern for the other varieties. Nor was there any observable relationship between temper and pottery type. Table 3 illustrates this fact. The χ^2 (chi square) test of association between temper and pottery type did yield a significant statistic, but the low Cramer's V, a measure of the strength of association between two variables, indicates that the empty cells affected the statistic. Thus, there is no evidence that temper and pottery type are related. What can be seen in Table 3 is the predominance of sand and sand and calcite tempering.

Table 3. Distribution of Temper by Pottery Type

TEMPUR	BURKETT S-COLLARED	BUTLER BRACED	NANCE FLARED DECORATED	WEBSTER BOWL WARE	WEBSTER COLLAR BRACED	WRIGHT COLLARED WARE	MISCELLANEOUS
SAND		9		2	7	6	7
GRIT						2	1
SAND & GRIT	1		1	1			2
SAND & CALCITE	1	1		2	7	9	3
SAND & HEMATITE		1				1	2
GRIT & SHERD				1			
CALCITE, LIMESTONE & SAND		1			3	2	
SHERD				1			

$\chi2 = 54.9553$ with 30 Degrees of Freedom, Significance $= 0.0036$, Cramer's V $= 0.43161$

The above statistics and table do not contain data from one Wright Collared Ware pot, two Nance Flared Decorated pots, and one Burkett S-Collared sherd which were on display and unavailable for examination.

TYPOLOGICAL CLASSIFICATION OF THE POTTERY

The ceramic assemblage was divided into four defined types and two wares using Grange's (1968:47-68) criteria. The types and wares present are Burkett S-Collared, Butler Braced, Nance Flared Decorated, Webster Bowl Ware, Webster Collar Braced, and Wright Collared Ware. Since these types and wares were defined primarily on the basis of rim form, only complete or nearly complete rims were useable for this study. From the total 124 sherds recovered by Smith's excavations in 1949, only 31 were rim sherds. Of these 31, only 16 were identifiable as to specific type. Figure 5 illustrates the types that were identified in the Smith collection. To augment this meager sample, the Kansas State Historical Society generously allowed the author to examine the rim sherds recovered during their excavations.

Among the several hundred rim sherds present in their collection, a total of 47 were identifiable. This brought the total sample of rim sherds to 63 identified specimens. Although this was not a large sample, it did allow the site to be used in a seriation of Historic Pawnee components.

Included among the sample of 63 are two complete pots, two reconstructed vessels, and three very large fragments. Thus, the analysis was not restricted to rim sherds, but also allowed statements to be made concerning body form, shoulder decoration, etc. in certain instances.

A type-by-type description of the major attributes recorded for the 63 rim sherds in the sample is set forth below. The miscellaneous/unidentified specimens from the assemblage Smith recovered are not included. To facilitate the understanding of these descriptions, several important points must be borne in mind. (1) "Rim Decoration" refers to purposefully produced designs restricted to or having a primary locus on the rim. No marks left by a construction technique, such as paddle marks, were considered designs. However, check stamping, which is probably part of the construction process, but occur only on the rim and not on associated body and shoulder sherds is considered to comprise a design motif. A pot with simple stamping on the body, shoulder and rim is classified as an undecorated rim because simple stamping is considered a common surface treatment, possibly part of the finishing process. A pot that is simple stamped on the shoulder and body but check stamped on the rim is classified as a decorated rim with a check stamped motif.

This classification is made because the check stamping represents a deliberate application of a given design to the rim area. Thus, the prime criteria for the identification of rim decoration are location (restricted to rim) and function (non-functional, not part of the construction process). (2) All measures of thickness and height were restricted to totally complete sherds. Thickness was not taken at pendant tabs. (3) "Color" is based on comparisons between the sherds and 17 selected color chips from the Munsell Soil Color Chart.

The sample size for each variable category within a type will vary due to problems with availability and preservation.

All variables are not applicable to each type and so only relevant variables are listed.

The following types and wares are present:

Burkett S-Collared

Burkett S-Collared sherds are recognizable by their "S" shaped rims.

Sample: 3 sherds.

Temper: See Table 3.

Vessel Form: There are no known specimens of Burkett S-Collared body or shoulder sherds.
Rim Decoration: See Table 4.
Lip Decoration: Two bear parallel-incised lines, one is undecorated.
Color: Pale brown, reddish yellow.
Lip Thickness: $N = 2$, $X = 4.5$mm, Range $= 4$-5mm.
Rim Thickness: $N = 2$, $X = 11$mm, Range $= 10$-12mm.
Rim Height: $N = 2$, $X = 37$mm, Range $= 30$-44mm.
Appendages: One specimen has a strap handle.

Table 4. Rim Motifs by Type.

Motif	Burkett S-Collared	Butler Braced	Nance Flared Decorated	Webster Bowl Ware	Webster Collar Braced	Wright Collared Ware	Miscellaneous
Indeterminate		1			2	2	12
Undecorated	1			6		1	2
⟪⟪⟪⟪⟪		3			3	3	
⟫⟫⟫⟫⟫			1		1		
(chevron motif)		1			6	4	
(chevron motif) Pinched Base					2		
(nested chevron motif)		1			1	4	1
(nested V motif)					1	1	
///////// iiiiiiiii	2	1				6	
(/ / / / motif)		4					
(hatched band motif)		1					
(finger impressions motif) Fingernail Impressions			1				
(radiating lines motif)			1				
(squares motif) Check Stamped					2		

$\chi2 = 123.97812$ with 55 Degrees of Freedom, Significance $= 0.0000$, Cramer's $V = 0.65384$

The above statistics are based solely on those cases where the rim motif and type were clearly discernible. No members of the miscellaneous/ unidentified category or those sherds with indeterminate motifs were included.

Butler Braced

Butler Braced (Figure 5d) sherds are recognizable by their wedge-shaped rims with slightly concave exterior surfaces. In rim height, Butler Braced sherds are greater than Colfax Braced specimens, but less than Wright Collared Ware rims (Grange1968: 60). This type is part of a transitional series wherein rim height increases. Butler Braced, Wright Collared Ware, and Webster Collared Braced represented the series (Grange personal communication).

Sample: 12 sherds.

Temper: See Table 3.

Vessel Form: No rim sherds are associated with shoulder or body sherds. Grange (1968:60) describes Butler Braced bodies as being "flattened, down-sloping upper body and rounded but fairly abrupt shoulder tapering to a rounded sub-conical base."

Rim Decoration: See Table 4.

Lip Decoration: Incised parallel lines are the most common. One sherd is punctated.

Color: Pale brown, grayish brown, dark gray.

Lip Thickness: $N = 12$, $X = 4.33$mm, Range $= 3$-6mm, Mode $= 4$mm.

Rim Thickness: $N = 11$, $X = 10.09$mm, Range $= 7$-14mm, Mode $= 8$mm.

Rim Height: $N = 12$, $X = 25.75$mm, Range $= 20$-33mm, Modes $= 20, 22, 23, 33$mm.

Rim Diameter: $N = 2$, $X = 110$mm, Range $= 100$-120mm.

Appendages: Strap handles are present on several specimens.

Nance Flared Decorated

Nance Flared Decorated sherds are identified by flaring or straight flared, uncollared rims with decoration present on the exterior surface.

Sample: 2 complete vessels and 1 rim sherd.

Temper: See Table 3.

Vessel Form: Both complete vessels are globular with round bottoms. The shoulder of one is sharply defined; the other's is more rounded. These complete specimens show that the neck could be either tightly constricted to produce an almost hourglass form, or it could be only slightly constricted to produce a more squat form. In both specimens the maximum body diameter exceeded the maximum rim diameter.

Rim Decoration: See Table 4.

Lip Decoration: The complete specimens have punctated lips. The incomplete rim is undecorated.

Shoulder Decoration: The complete specimens have incised line decorations. The specimen with the herringbone motif on its rim has a design on its shoulder similar to the rim motif of the other complete vessel (see Table 4). The latter pot's shoulder is incised with part of the rim motif, i.e. the rim decoration intrudes onto the shoulder.

Body Decoration: The shoulder decoration on the vessel with the herringbone pattern on the rim extends below onto the body proper. The other vessel has parallel-incised diagonal lines, upper right to lower left, on its body.

Color: Grayish brown.

Lip Thickness: $N = 1$, $X = 8$mm.

Rim Thickness: $N = 1$, $X = 10$mm.

Appendages: A squat specimen with the "sunburst" motif has two opposing strap handles.

Webster Bowl Ware

Webster Bowl Ware (Figure 5e and f) is recognizable as small hemispherical bowls, usually poorly made. Red pigment is commonly associated with this type and traces are present on four of the six sherds present in the collection.

Sample: 5 sherds and one large fragment.

Temper: See Table 3. The temper is usually very sparse.

Vessel Form: Hemispherical bowls. The bottoms were probably rounded, based on a reconstruction of a vessel from a large fragment. Most of the specimens exhibit what Grange (1968:45) calls "a carelessly made appearance."

Lip Decoration: Decoration, per se, is not present on any specimens. Two sherds are simple stamped; one is smoothed over. One sherd has a single vertically oriented fingernail impression. It is not known if this forms part of a motif or an unintentional impression left by the potter.

Color: Pale brown, grayish brown, and very dark gray.
Lip Thickness: N = 6, X = 5.67mm, Range = 4-7mm, Modes = 4, 6, 7mm.
Rim Diameter: N = 1, X = 100mm.
Body Thickness: N = 3, X = 13.33, Range = 7-25mm.
Appendages: There are no associated appendages.

Webster Collar Braced

Webster Collar Braced (Figure 5a) is recognizable by its high, collared rim that is braced (solid) rather than channeled. This is the most common pottery type present on historic Pawnee sites (Grange 1968:61).

Sample: 18 sherds.
Temper: See Table 3.
Vessel Form: There are no associated body sherds and only one rounded shoulder sherd. Grange (1968:61-2) describes Webster Collar Braced vessels as having the collar braced rim extending out over a constricted neck. "Globular bodies with rounded shoulders and bases are present, but a slightly flattened, sloping, rounded shoulder and a tapering body with a rounder sub-conical base is more frequent."
Rim Decoration: See Table 4.
Lip Decoration: Parallel incised lines are the most common. There is a low incidence of notching, punctating, and plain lips.
Color: Gray, pale brown.
Lip Thickness: N = 18, X = 5.56mm, Range = 4-8mm, Mode = 5mm.
Rim Thickness: N = 17, X = 12.94mm, Range = 8-17mm, Mode = 16mm.
Rim Height: N = 18, X = 42.17mm, Range = 26-53mm, Mode = 46mm.
Rim Diameter: N = 2, X = 110mm, Range = 100-120mm.
Shoulder Thickness: N = 1, X = 11mm.
Appendages: Pendant tabs were present on most specimens. There is evidence of strap handles on several specimens.

Wright Collared Ware

Wright Collared Ware (Figs. 5b, 5c, and 6) is recognizable by its characteristic deep channel on the interior of its collared rim.

Sample: 2 restored vessels, 19 rim sherds.
Temper: See Table 3.

Figure 6. Reconstructed Wright Collared Ware Pot.

Vessel Form: The collared rim overhangs a constricted neck. The body is globular with rounded shoulders and a rounded bottom. The maximum diameter of the pot is just below the shoulder and is greater than the rim diameter.

Rim Decoration: See Table 4.

Lip Decoration: Parallel incised lines are the most common, some are undecorated, and one is punctated.

Shoulder Decoration: All associated shoulder sherds are simple stamped.

Body Decoration: All associated body sherds are simple stamped.

Color: Pale to grayish browns, dark gray, light red, and reddish yellow.

Lip Thickness: N = 13, X = 4.6mm, Range = 2-6mm, Mode = 5mm.

Rim Thickness: N = 18, X = 13.67mm, Range = 8-43mm, Mode = 9mm.

Rim Height: N = 15, X = 32.05mm, Range = 28-51mm, Mode = 36mm.

Rim Diameter: N = 3, X = 121.67mm, Range = 85-140mm, Mode = 140mm.

Shoulder Thickness: N = 3, X = 9.3mm, Range = 7-11mm.

Body Thickness: N = 2, X = 7.5mm, Range = 7-8mm.

Appendages: Pendant tabs are present on most specimens. Several fragments have strap handles or evidence for such handles.

Body Sherds (including shoulder sherds)

Sample: 93 sherds.

Temper: 42 sand-tempered, 40 sand and calcite, 4 grit, 4 sand and grit, 2 grit and hematite.

Vessel Form: All complete or reconstructed pots indicate that a globular body with a normally well-defined shoulder, and a rounded bottom was the most common form.

Surface Finish: Twenty-two sherds were simple stamped. There is a low incidence of polishing present in the sample. No incised designs are identifiable in the sample.

Color: Pale brown is the most common, followed by grayish brown, dark gray and reddish yellow. There were lower incidence of light brown, very dark gray, very pale brown, and red.

Shoulder Thickness: N = 2, X = 9.5mm, Range = 8-11mm.

Body Thickness: N = 51, X = 7.7mm, Range = 1-13mm, Mode = 8mm.

THE HISTORIC PAWNEE CERAMIC SERIATION

One of the first things revealed by this typological analysis is the considerable variation between the findings and the ceramic assemblage described by Grange (1968:79). The published account reports 90% Webster Collar Braced, 8% Nance Straight Plain and 1% Colfax Braced. The lack of correspondence is the result of Grange basing his classification of the material on just a few sherds in the Nebraska State Historical Society Museum and Smith's (1950) published descriptions of the pottery (Grange personal communication). Since Smith's publication predates the definition of these types, the descriptions contained therein cause errors when the material is typed without personal examination. In order to eliminate the possibility that the variability was due to classifier error, samples from the assemblage were shown to Grange. He agreed with the classifications in all instances. Thus, this analysis will proceed using the six types just defined.

The greatest impact this analysis has is on the seriation of Historic Pawnee sites developed by Grange. The impact is so great that the entire seriation must be reconsidered in light of the new findings. Though revision is necessary, the end result is actually a strengthening of the seriation.

It is obvious that the Kansas Monument site with an assemblage composed of 33.3% Wright Collared Ware, 28.6% Webster Collar Braced, 19% Butler Braced, 9.5% Webster Bowl Ware, 4.8% Burkett S-Collared, and 4.8% Nance Flared Decorated, does not belong in the position it currently occupies in the Lower Loup-Pawnee ceramic seriation (Grange 1968:105, 115). The assemblage illustrated in Grange's seriation graph is heavy in Webster Collar Braced sherds, a ceramic type that is common in late Pawnee sites. Since most of the types identified in this project are not common in late sites, the Kansas Monument site must occupy an earlier position in the seriation sequence.

It was decided to re-seriate the Pawnee sites used by Grange. The Meighan (1959) three-pole method was selected as the most direct means of seriation. A major problem presented itself immediately when the re-seriation was begun. Of the 13 historic Pawnee sites used by Grange, only seven had more than 50 rim sherds. Grange (1968:78) noted that the use of sites or excavation units with less than 50 sherds did not conform to Ford's (1949:36) guidelines, but decided to include them to examine trends in the seriation. The author feels that the use of sites with small samples, some as low as three, would and did have an adverse effect on the seriation. Therefore, only sites where the number of rim sherds exceeds 50 will be used in this re-seriation.

The seven sites with sufficiently large samples are the Palmer site (25HW1), the Blue Springs site (25GA1), the Linwood site (25BU1), the Bellwood site (25BU2), the Hill site (25WT1), the Horse Creek site (25NC2) and the Kansas Monument site. Table 5 provides the raw count data for the seven most common ceramic types at each site, as reported by Grange (1968:79-100). These data will be used to construct the seriation graphs.

Table 5. Distribution of Seven Pottery Types among Seven Historic Pawnee Sites

TYPE	14RP1	25BU1	25BU2	25GA1	25HW1	25NC2	25WT1
Nance Flared Plain	0	13	2	7	4	10	16
Nance Flared Decorated	3	16	9	7	6	2	18
Wright Collared Ware	18	1	0	0	1	1	6
Colfax Braced	0	7	3	0	5	1	4
Butler Braced	11	1	0	1	1	2	1
Webster Collar Braced	18	61	37	18	18	166	176
Webster Bowl Ware	4	0	2	9	12	21	120

Figure 7 shows the results of a seriation based on percentages of Nance Flared Decorated, Webster Collar Braced, and Wright Collared Ware. Figure 8 shows the results of a seriation based on the percentages of Nance Flared Plain and Decorated combined, Webster Collar Braced and Webster Bowl Ware combined, and Wright Collared Ware. Note in both instances the Kansas Monument site (14RP1) is the earliest and the Horse Creek site (25NC2) and the Hill site (25WT1) are the latest sites. Table 6 compares the results of these seriations against Grange's seriation.

Figure 7. Triangular Plot Seriation of Seven Historic Pawnee Sites.

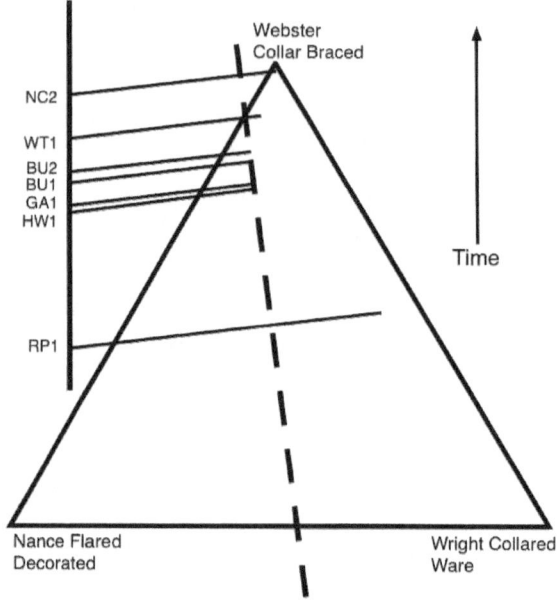

Figure 8. Triangular Plot of Seven Historic Pawnee Sites.

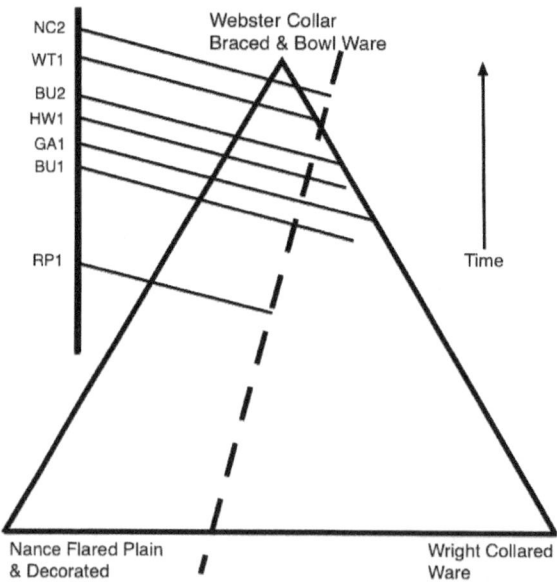

Included in Table 6 are site orderings based on midpoints of occupation dates. The occupation spans were derived from historical sources and are documented in Grange (1968:19-26, 117-121). An additional set of

46

orderings was derived from the ceramic formula dating system Grange (1974, 1977) developed from the system originally devised by South (1972). In both of these orderings the position of the Kansas Monument site is based on the new evidence advanced in this paper.

Table 6. Site Orderings.

GRANGE'S SERIATION	SERIATION #1	SERIATION #2
14RP1	25NC2	25NC2
25NC2	25WT1	25WT1
25BU2	25BU2	25BU2
25BU1	25BU1	25HW1
25WT1	25GA1	25GA1
25GA1	25HW1	25BU1
25HW1	14RP1	14RP1

OCCUPATION MIDPOINT	FORMULA DATES
25NC2 (1825.0)	25WT1 (1824.6 ± 23)
25HW1 (1820.0)	25NC2 (1814.6 ± 39)
25GA1 (1811.0)	25BU2 (1809.1 ± 32)
25BU2 (1798.5)	25BU1 (1806.2 ± 30)
25BU1 (1793.0)	25HW1 (1791.6 ± 57)
25WT1 (1792.5)	25GA1 (1783.5 ± 65)
14RP1 (1777.0)*	14RP1 (1776.0 ± 48)**

*This midpoint is based on documentary sources combined with *formula dates*.

**The date is based on the ceramic assemblage reported in this paper, *not that of Grange's*.

The conclusion drawn from these comparisons is that the Kansas Monument site is earlier in time than is now currently believed. Table 7 provides ceramic formula dates for each major excavation unit at the site. These dates point to an occupation in the 1770's. Documentary sources record the presence of a Pawnee band on the Republican River in 1777 (Houck 1909:143; Nasatir 1952:70; also see Wedel 1936:15 for a discussion of the locations mentioned in these sources).

Table 7. Ceramic Formula Dates for Major Excavation Units at 14RP1.

UNIT	DATE
HOUSE 1	1768.5 + 47
HOUSE 2	1781.8 + 53
HOUSE 3	1760.0 + 14
HOUSE 5	1804.0 + 0
HOUSE 6	1825.0 + 0
HOUSE 7	1825.0 + 0
HOUSE 24	1768.3 + 49
HOUSE 25	1768.3 + 49
PIT SW OF HOUSE 5	1773.8 + 32
PIT W OF HOUSE 3	1787.9 + 64
A652, A666, &	
FEATURE 7	1776.8 + 54
A661	1785.0 + 35
A665	1825.0 + 0
A673	1760.0 + 0
FEATURE 2	1740.0 + 0
ALL HOUSES	1771.0 + 20
SITE TOTAL	**1775.96 + 48**

Thus, in this test of Hypothesis 1, the ceramics indicate a definite early occupation for the site. Evidence for a late occupation is tenuous, based solely on the formula dates. If a late occupation is present, Houses 6, 7 and possibly 4 and 5, all excavated by Witty, represent it. These are low in the number of identifiable sherds, one for 5, 6, and 7 and none for 4. A low number of identifiable sherds do not reflect a low incidence of pottery, however. If these houses also have a lower frequency of ceramics than the other houses, then that would be considered good evidence that they were occupied late in time, since a low incidence of pottery is typical of late sites.

The formula dates also allow the only opportunity currently available to test Hypothesis 2. This Hypothesis states that benched houses are indicative of a late period in time. House 3 and House 7 are benched earthlodges; the remainders of the excavated houses are unbenched. The formula date for House 3 is 1760.0 ± 14 years and for House 7, 1825.0 ± 0. The House 3 date is based on a sample of four including 2 complete pots, and the House 7 date is based on a sample of one sherd. Thus, it can be concluded that benching is not a temporal indicator. Hypothesis 2 cannot be supported by the data in this thesis.

A STUDY OF ASSOCIATION AMONG SELECT CERAMIC VARIABLES FROM THE POTTERY ASSEMBLAGE

Grange, in his study, was unable to detect band differences on the basis of ceramic types alone. He is currently working on the problem of using rim motifs to distinguish among bands (Grange personal communication). An analysis of the distribution of rim motifs within the site has implications for Grange's larger scale project. If it is demonstrated that a given design is strongly associated with a given feature, particularly a house, then it may be possible to use that design to (1) trace movements of the band to which the potter who produced the design belonged and (2) thereby to identify a given band archaeologically.

Using the SPSS (Nie et al. 1975) program, CROSSTABS, rim motif was compared against location (Table 8). As can be seen in the statistics at the end of the table, the $\chi 2$ statistic indicates that rim motif and location are not independent of each other. It is noted that the number of cells with zero or low numbers less than five can affect the $\chi 2$ statistic. A measure of the strength of association between two variables not affected by zero cells, Cramer's V, is included in this table as a control for the $\chi 2$ (Doran and Hodson 1975:147). In this way, a significant $\chi 2$ would also have a high Cramer's V. Thus, the data in Table 6 do indicate a relationship between rim motif and location. Cramer's V is not very high and so the author hesitates to push the conclusions too far.

Table 8. Distribution of Rim Motif by Major Excavation Unit.

Motif	H. 1	H. 2	H. 3	H. 5	H. 6	H. 7	H. 24	H. 25	Pit SW of H. 5	Pit W of H. 3	A652 A666 Fea. 7	A661	A665	A673	Fea. 2
Indeterminate	2	1								1	2				
Undecorated	2	1						1		1	3				
⟨⟨⟨⟨⟨							1	1	3	2	2				
⟩⟩⟩⟩⟩		1									1				
(hatched herringbone)	3			1			1	1	1	1	1	2			
(hatched herringbone) Pinched Base											1				
(nested triangles)		3	1								1				1
(chevron down)		1				1									
///////	1	1	1										5	1	
//// (with loops)	1			1						4					
(hatched band)				1											
∩∩∩∩ Fingernail Impressions													1		
(radiating lines)				1											
(squares) Check Stamped								1	1						

$\chi2 = 231.23194$ with 15 Degrees of Freedom, Significance $= 0.0000$, Cramer's $V = 0.60202$

The above statistics are based solely on sherds with identifiable rim motifs. No indeterminate motif sherds were included.

Aside from those motifs which occur only once, there are several apparently significant associations: the herringbone motif is strongly associated with the two cache pits and the midden area behind House 2 (A652, A666, and Feature 7); the diagonal line with vertical terminus motif is also related to the midden area; and the diagonal line with fingernail terminus motif is restricted to the cache pit southwest of House 5. Unfortunately, there is a lack of evidence to suggest a relationship between any of the motifs and any of the houses. Among the hundreds of rim sherds in the Kansas State Historical Society's collection there are many with identifiable rim motifs even though the sherd itself cannot be classified as to type. If these data were added to those that have already been compiled about the complete sherds, it may be possible to isolate particular motifs that correlate well with a given house.

The implication from the above analysis is that certain rim motifs are more strongly associated with certain parts of the site than others. The corollary to this is if rim motifs are restrictively distributed within a village, they may also be restrictively distributed between villages. Thus, rim motifs may eventually be useful in differentiating archaeologically between Pawnee bands. One caution should be noted in pursuing this goal, however. As Wedel (1936: 68) pointed out, there is a great deal of uniformity in Pawnee designs on pottery. There will be a number of designs that are common to nearly all Pawnee sites. The important designs will be those that are not common, the ones that are most likely to be the function of a potter's idiosyncratic behavior. If these idiosyncratic designs can be isolated, then they may be the most useful ones in identifying bands. In short, the ultimate approach to using rim motifs to differentiate between bands is not to define motifs diagnostic of a band, per se, because this may not be possible, but rather to identify those motifs diagnostic of a potter, or potters, within the band.

The analysis indicates that certain motifs tend to occur in certain parts of the site to the exclusion of other areas. The explanation for this occurrence suggests that a given design can be favored by a potter and thus tend to occur in the area where the potter lives, does her work, or disposes of her trash. Attention should be paid to whether other variables have particular distributions within the site. A potter could favor some other attribute besides rim motif. Some of the other variable distributions are explored below.

In Table 4 rim motif and pottery type are tested for independence. As can be seen, the χ^2 statistic indicates that the two are not independent. Cramer's V in this instance is higher than it was above. An examination of the table shows the following: Webster Bowl Ware sherds are not decorated; the herringbone design is almost exclusively associated with three types, Butler Braced, Wright Collared Ware, and Webster Collar Braced. This is particularly interesting because, as was noted earlier, these three types form a transitional series. The filled-in triangular plats correlate with Webster Collar Braced sherds; Wright Collared Ware has a strong association with the chevron separated by horizontal lines motif and the diagonal with vertical terminus motif; and the diagonal line with fingernail terminus motif is exclusively associated with Butler Braced sherds. The implication of the above findings is twofold: (1) a potter may not only favor a given rim motif, but might also favor a particular pottery type, or (2) regardless of who the potter is, certain motifs may be reserved for particular types of pots. The test of these implications necessitates a stylistic investigation beyond the scope of this paper.

Rim motifs have definable distributions within the site and there are strong correlations between design and type, the distribution of the types themselves is tested. Table 9 shows the distribution of pottery types by major excavation unit. Again the χ^2 is significant but in this instance Cramer's V is not very high. This low Cramer's V raises the question of the strength of association between the variables. Since this is the total sample of identifiable specimens from the site, additional data cannot be secured without further excavations. Therefore, although the evidence is suggestive of a relationship between type and location, the author does not feel that the data can support the drawing of any conclusions about what that relationship might be.

Table 9. Distribution of Pottery Types by Major Excavation Unit.

Location	Burkett S-Collar	Butler Braced	Nance Flared Decorated	Webster Bowl Ware	Webster Collar Braced	Wright Collared Ware	Miscellaneous
House 1		1		2		5	4
House 2				2	1	4	7
House 3		1	2			1	
House 5	1						
House 6					1		
House 7					1		
House 24					1	2	
House 25					1	2	
Pit SW of House 5		5			2	1	
Pit W of House 3	1	1			4		
A652, A666 & Feature 7	1	2		2	4	5	1
A661		1	1		1		
A665					2		
A673		1					
Feature 2						1	2
TOTAL	**3**	**12**	**3**	**6**	**18**	**21**	**15***

$\chi 2 = 100.84258$ with 70 Degrees of Freedom, Significance $= 0.0078$, Cramer's $V = 0.56137$

The above statistics are based solely on identified sherds and do not include specimens in the miscellaneous/ unidentified category.

*Includes one sherd of unknown provenience.

DISCUSSION

This section has been most pertinent to the goals of this thesis. It is only through ceramics that the Kansas Monument site can be accurately compared with other Historic Pawnee sites. It is also only the ceramics that allow comparisons among all the houses that have been excavated.

In this section, Hypotheses 1 and 2 were tested. The ceramic assemblage from the site indicates that the occupation was most likely during the

1770's. This conclusion is supported by the documentary data. There was also evidence to suggest a late occupation in the 1820's. A final determination as to whether there was a late occupation awaits an in-depth evaluation of all the artifacts from the houses involved.

The formula dates for the houses do not support the hypothesis that late houses were benched. Time is not the factor that determines whether or not a house is benched. An examination of the distribution of rim motifs through the site indicates that certain motifs are restrictively distributed among the houses. From this fact, it is postulated that a motif restrictively distributed within a village may also be restrictively distributed among villages, thus serving as a marker for a given band. The identification of bands using rim motifs as a criterion would be most successful if the focus is on identifying the motif(s) of a given potter within a band rather than attempting to identify motifs diagnostic of a band, *per se*.

LITHIC ARTIFACTS

Lithics comprise one of the largest artifact categories at the Kansas Monument site. The most common lithic artifacts are scrapers and shaft smoothers. Most of the material contained in this section represents traditional Pawnee produced goods. However, this section also includes gunflints, a category that represents a traditional behavior being adapted to a new purpose.

SCRAPERS

There are four different varieties of scrapers present. They are distinguished on the basis of size, shape, and whether or not they were made on flakes.

Hafted Scrapers (Figure 9d and e). These scrapers are differentiated from the others because they are smaller than the other scrapers and are made from flakes. They are the only specimens with evidence of having been hafted. Both are made from the mottled grayish-blue chert typical of the Florence formation. Two specimens: Length - 44, 55mm; Width - 32, 38mm; Thickness - 9, 10mm.

Both specimens could be classified as end scrapers, although specimen 14055 (Figure 9d) does show its heaviest use scars on the laterals. Some consideration was given to reclassifying the specimen as a knife. The other specimen is an example of the planoconvex endscraper Wedel (1936:76) says occurs only rarely except for early sites. This scraper has a concave working surface on the end.

Both specimens have hafting elements that expand slightly from the base of the scraper. In the case of the scraper from House 1 (Figure 9d) the working edge constricts. The planoconvex scraper from House 2 has an expanding working edge, but there is a definite break between the expansion of the hafting element and the edge expansion. In addition, the planoconvex specimen has a hinge fracture on the proximal end indicating that it snapped while hafted. The scarring present on the hinge fracture is probably the result of box retouch rather than special modification or use.

Given a larger sample, these two scrapers might be separated. It was decided to leave them in a single class because they have more in common with each other than they do with any of the other lithic artifacts.

Figure 9. Lithic Artifacts: a. Expanding Scraper; b. Eliptical Scraper; c. Discoidal Scraper; d. & e. Hafted Scrapers; f. Possibly Re-Worked Projectile Point Fragment; g. Aboriginal Gunflint; h. European Gunspall; i. Biface Fragment.

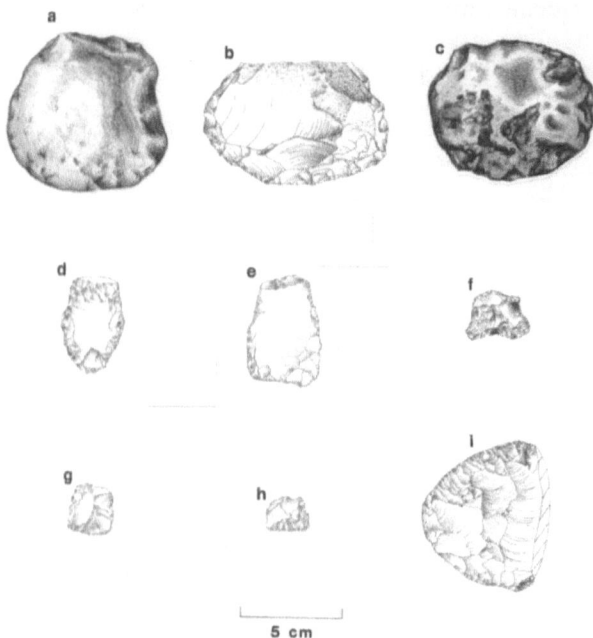

5 cm

Expanding Scrapers (Figure 9a). Four artifacts, two from each lodge, are heavy scrapers termed expanding scrapers. A flat base, expanding laterals, and a convex working edge characterize these pieces. Three of the four specimens have flat un-beveled laterals. The fourth scraper has had one of its sides modified by rough chipping and grinding to continue the working edge around, almost to the base. Three of the scrapers are made from fine-grained sandstone. These vary in length from 91-78mm, in width from 78-75mm, and in thickness from 27-14mm. The thickest point is at the base. From this point, thickness decreases at an even rate down to the working edge. One side of each of these three pieces has been ground almost flat, so that in profile they resemble wedges. The fourth specimen is much larger than the rest. It is made from an Ogallala quartzite flake and has a length of 159mm, a width of 83mm, and a maximum thickness of 23mm. The base of this piece is also somewhat more rounded than the flat bases of the other specimens.

Scrapers such as these were likely used in dressing hides. The flat base would have allowed the user to hold the piece in his hand without being injured. The grinding may have been the result of use as abraders as well as scrapers.

Elliptical Scrapers (Figure 9b). Nine lithic artifacts, one from House 1 and eight from House 2, are examples of the type Wedel (1936:76) terms elliptical scrapers. An almost elliptical shape characterizes these scrapers with one side more or less flattened. The working edge usually extends all the way around except for the flat side. On six of the specimens the working edge extends from the flattened side only a little over halfway around (see Figure 9b). The remainder has been left unaltered or has been flattened to produce a finger rest. This suggests that the tool was held in the hand with the working edge in a vertical position rather than horizontal. Such a position would be more conducive to chopping and sawing behavior rather than pushing or pulling normally associated with scraping behavior.

Seven of the scrapers are made from fine-grained sandstone, two are made from quartzite from the Dakota formation, and one is made from the chert that comes from the Florence formation. The chert scraper is made on a large flake modified by knapping only. Both crude chipping and grinding have modified the remainder of the pieces. Several pieces exhibit ground surfaces that suggest they were used as abraders rather than ground for modification. Measuring length from the flat side to the opposite working edge, the pieces vary from 101-58mm. They vary in width from 127-88mm and in thickness from 44-22mm. It can be seen in these numbers that these pieces tend to be wider than they are long. These scrapers are common on Historic Pawnee sites, rare on protohistoric sites, and absent pre-historically (Wedel 1936:76).

Discoidal Scrapers (Figure 9c). Five specimens, three from House 1 and two from House 2 are classified as discoidal scrapers. Their roughly circular or elliptical shape distinguishes these scrapers with a working edge that extends all the way round the circumference. All of the specimens were made from a fine-grained sandstone by crude chipping and grinding. Four of the five have an elliptical cross-section, the fifth is double beveled and so has a cross-section like a harahey knife. The maximum diameter varies between 122 and 83mm. The thickness varies between 34 and 26mm.

BIFACE

No complete bifaces were recovered from the site. The only bifacial specimen is a fragment of a blade. Such pieces may have been used as knives but shall not be so called here because of the lack of evidence.

Biface Fragment (Figure 9i). A finely made biface fragment made from chert out of the Florence formation was found in House 1. There is evidence of use on the tip and sides. Whether the piece was used prior to breaking cannot be determined. The blade was definitely used after it broke. Use has worn down one side of the piece into the break. Since the wear is directly at the junction of the working edge with the break, the piece may have been used for graving or some similar activity. Opposite the worn edge is a fossil inclusion, probably responsible for the break. The thickness and lack of evenness for the working edge on this side suggests that the piece may have broken during thinning.

GUNFLINTS

Gunflints are the only nonmetal gun parts to survive at the Kansas Monument site. Gunflints can be separated on the basis whether they are of European or aboriginal manufacture. The determination of origin of the flints is based on material of manufacture and form.

Aboriginal Gunflints (Figure 9g). Five of the seven gunflints recovered at the site are classified as aboriginal. Included in these five is the flint clamped in the jaws of the flintlock mechanism from House 1. All five specimens were manufactured from non-European chert and exhibit knapping techniques such as pressure retouch not used by Europeans. Three of the flints are from House 1 and two from House 2. One flint from each house is made from a material not locally obtained - Alibates chert. This multicolored mottled chert is available only from a quarry site in the Texas panhandle (Shaeffer 1958). As a raw material, Alibates chert was popular in the aboriginal trade long before contact. These Alibates specimens do not appear to have been modified from any other type of tool. The specimen from House 2 (Figure 9g) even appears to be copied from the form of French gunflints (compare with Smith 1960, Figure 13). Excluding the flint in the cock, the aboriginal flints have the following measurements: Length - 27 to 24mm; Width - 29 to 23mm; and Maximum Thickness - 8 to 6mm.

European Gunflints (Figure 9h). Two specimens, both from House 1, are identified as European gunflints. One specimen is a broken flint (the narrow end has broken off). The other is a planoconvex flint more commonly called a gunspall. The broken flint has been burned to a chalky white but the heel indicates that it is a French flint (Smith 1960). The gunspall is a grayish tan flint that is considered to be French in origin. Such a specimen as this would be used most probably in a small fowling piece. The flint has been modified on the striking edge by pressure retouch, probably to resharpen it. Maxwell and Binford (1961:99-100) report that gunspalls such as this were popular throughout both the French and English occupation of Fort Michilimackinac. From the heel to the striking edge the spall measures 17mm. The striking edge is 22mm wide. At the bulb of percussion the flint is 6mm thick.

HAMMERSTONES

Two varieties of hammerstones are present at the Kansas Monument site in addition to the pecking stones described below. The different varieties are separated on the basis of form and probable function.

Cobble Hammerstones (Figure 10b). Two specimens of cobble hammerstones were recovered from House 2. Both are made of quartzite, one is Ogallala quartzite; the other is an unknown variety of water worn quartzite. Each has been battered to form a flat area along the circumference. Directly opposite the flat area on each piece is a heavily pitted surface. There is also a slightly concave face on both hammerstones. Both pieces show battering all the way around the outer edge.

Figure 10. Lithic Artifacts: a. Discoidal Hammerstone; b. Cobble Hammerstone; c. Stone Ball; d. Pecking Stone; e. Grooved Maul; f. Amorphous Grinding Slab; g. Ovoid Grinding Slab.

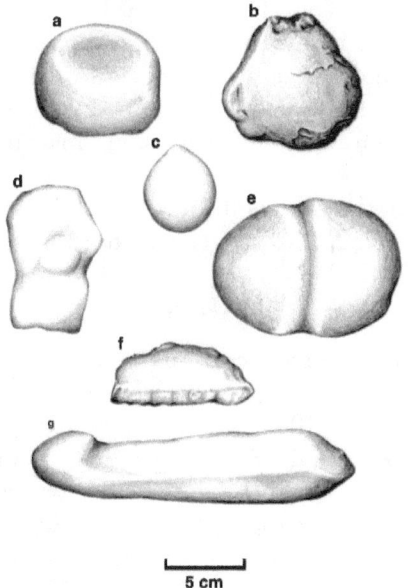

5 cm

Discoidal Hammerstones (Figure 10a). These circular hammerstones have concave faces for gripping. Three of the four specimens have one section of the edge flatter than the remainder. The area where the face joins the edge is rounded in all specimens. These latter two characteristics are rare for hammerstones of this form (Wedel 1936:76). Two specimens were recovered from each house. All are quartzite with diameters of 82-119mm and thicknesses of 53-69mm. The largest specimen from each house has at least one of the concave faces impregnated with a red material probably hematite, suggesting that they may have had a dual function - serving as both hammerstone and mortar in mineral processing.

PECKING STONES

Carlson (1973:71) identified a stone ball similar to that described in this thesis as a pecking stone. A similar classification did not hold with the Kansas Monument specimen for the reasons discussed. There is, however, a true pecking stone at the site.

Pecking Stone (Figure 10d). This artifact is an oddly shaped piece of the same fine-grained yellow sandstone from which the stone ball was made. This piece is termed a pecking stone because it has only one area of battering. Directly opposite the pitted area is a flattened area, possibly representing a finger rest. There are two grooves or depressions on the piece, one on either side. These depressions appear to be the result of wear rather than pecking or grinding. If this stone is held with the length axis in a vertical position, with the index finger resting on the purported finger rest, then the thumb and third finger fit perfectly into the depressions on their respective sides. This sandstone can be abraded with one's fingers without much difficulty. Therefore, these depressions may be the result of the user's handling of the stone.

This piece has a maximum length of 93mm. Its width is 63mm. The maximum thickness is 42mm. It was recovered from House 2.

MAULS

Two grooved mauls were recovered. The larger of the two may actually be a preform.

Grooved Mauls (Figure 10e). The two grooved maul specimens were both recovered from House 1. The larger maul is made from Ogallala quartzite. It is in poor condition because of fire cracking. The groove is wide and shallow and does not appear to go all the way around; this may be due to distortion from the fire cracking. This specimen shows very little evidence of battering - only on the wider end. The apparent lack of use, coupled with the incomplete groove and the size of the piece, suggest that it may be only a preform.

The small maul is of quartzite and has a groove all the way around although on one side the groove becomes almost negligible. There is evidence of heavy battering on both ends. This maul has a length of 120mm, a width of 89mm, and a thickness of 64mm. The large maul has a length of 133mm but the other measurements would be misleading due to its condition. Mauls such as these are very common in historic Pawnee sites.

STONE BALLS

Stone Ball (Figure 10c). A single specimen was recovered from House 2. This ball is made from a fine-grained yellow sandstone and has a maximum diameter of 53mm. There is a node on the ball that shows signs of battery, indicating that these balls were made by pecking. Grinding subsequent to the pecking would have removed the overall evidence. These balls are of unknown function and are common in historic Pawnee sites but are usually found in graves. Carlson (1973: 71; Figure XB, 13) describes and illustrates a similar specimen identified as a pecking stone. He may have an example similar to this one, wherein the evidence of the initial pecking to produce the form has not been obliterated.

MANOS AND METATES

The occurrence of manos and metates in Pawnee sites is rare (Wedel 1936:74-5). However, one specimen of each was identified.

Metate (Figure 11e). The single stone metate is an almost rectangular piece of dark fine-grained sandstone. The piece is 200mm long, 175mm wide and has a maximum thickness of 66mm. Both surfaces are smooth but one is much smoother and has been worn down to a slight concavity by apparent grinding activity. This metate was recovered from Feature 1, a cache pit, where it was in association with seven scapula hoes.

Mano (Figure 11b). An ovoid piece of very coarse-grained sandstone has been classified a mano. This piece is from House 2. It has a flat face that would be used in grinding. The opposite surface is convex and slopes from the middle towards both ends to facilitate it being held in the hand. The piece measures 155mm along the longitudinal axis, 85mm in width, and has a maximum thickness of 56mm. An additional specimen described in the section on grinding palettes may have seen use as a mano or other abrading instrument.

Figure 11. Ground Stone: a. Mortar; b. Mano; c. Metate.

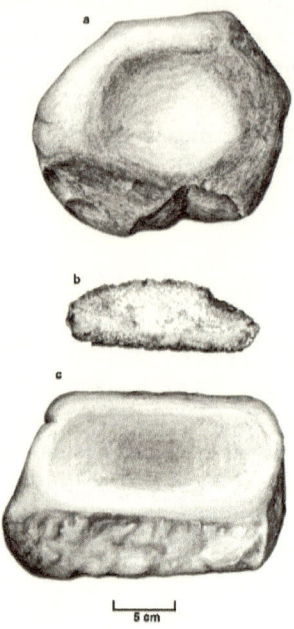

MORTARS

In the literature stone mortars have often been referred to as anvil stones. It was decided that anvil stone is not an appropriate term for these artifacts because it is now most commonly used to refer to large stones used in knapping flint. The anvil stones reported by Wedel and Strong were used in the food preparation process for pounding and grinding meat during the storage process (Wedel 1936:75). Therefore, it was decided to refer to these artifacts as mortars, the same term applied to their wooden counterparts.

Stone Mortar (Figure 11a). Only one stone mortar was recovered from House 1. This single specimen is made from a large, roughly rectangular piece of Ogallala quartzite. It has a maximum length of 198mm, a maximum width of 166mm, and a maximum thickness of 77mm. The presumed surface of primary use is visibly pitted, but has been abraded to a very smooth texture. This surface is concave with a maximum depth of 10mm. The opposite surface has a slight concavity, but is in a very rough state, showing no sign of smoothing.

The Pawnee used wooden pestles with both stone and wooden mortars. No pestles were recovered.

GRINDING PALETTES

Pieces that have been used as grinding surfaces are termed Palettes. Specimens are sorted on the basis of shape, which also appears to define function. Given further data, these different categories may be integrated to form a single variety.

Amorphous Grinding Slabs (Figure 10f). This class is composed of two irregularly shaped pieces of ground stone. There is some degree of grinding present on all surfaces, but there is one face on each specimen that was clearly the primary work surface. It has been considered that these artifacts may be fragments of larger more regularly shaped pieces, however both show wear on all edges indicating use in their present state. Both pieces bear stains of a red mineral on their primary working surface. The specimen from House 1 (Figure 12f) has its entire working surface and most of the edge stained with the red pigment. The specimen from Trench 4 in the fortification wall is not as heavily stained. The presence of this staining may indicate that artifacts are paint-grinding slabs (Carlson 1973:72) seems best to use only the criteria of form until further evidence is available on the function of grinding slabs. The measurements for the slabs from House 1 and the fortification wall are: Length - 93, 99; Width - 54, 87; Thickness - 18, 26mm.

Ovoid Grinding Slab (Figure 10g). A single specimen of Dakota quartzite from House 2 has been designated as an ovoid grinding slab. In the original catalogue for this piece it was described as a mano, a term not used here because of the manner in which the piece was ground as described above. This piece is 211mm long, 94mm wide and 37mm thick. It has a roughly oval shape. One surface has been ground down to form a trough. The opposite surface has been ground slightly so that it is smooth to the touch over about half of the surface area. The grinding on the latter face, however, was not of sufficient duration or intensity to form a concave surface. There are no remains present on the surface to suggest what was being ground.

SHAFT SMOOTHERS

These form one of the largest single stone artifact groups in the collection. The large number of specimens is due to the fact that all are fragments or are reconstructed from fragments.

Boat-Shaped Shaft Smoothers (Figure 12a). A total of 19 reconstructed or fragmentary shaft smoothers were recovered. Only one specimen, a fragment, came from House 1. Two additional fragments came from the north side of the fortification wall. The remainder of the specimens came from House 2. All of the pieces are made from Dakota sandstone and vary in color from brownish yellow to grayish red to grey.

There is no evidence that any of the fragments vary from the traditional boat shape with flat ends, flat top, and round bottom. The groove in each smoother ran longitudinally. Three specimens were constructed or found complete. The measurements for these artifacts are as follows: Length - 106, 101, 93; Width - 32, 39, 34; Thickness - 19, 22, 22mm. The second specimen in the above measures appears to have been broken and then re-modified. Thus, its original length and width may have been larger. Several of the fragments were utilized as abraders, leaving their grooves sometimes only faintly visible and reducing their round bottoms to flat surfaces. Shaft polishers are not unusual on historic Pawnee sites. They usually occur in pairs but this cannot be documented in this collection.

Figure 12. Ground Stone: a. Shaft Straightener; b. Whetstone; c. Abrader; d. unidentified Ground Stone; e. Elbow Pipe; f. Pipe Preform; g. Pottery Working Tool (?); h. Elbow Pipe; i. Pipe Preform.

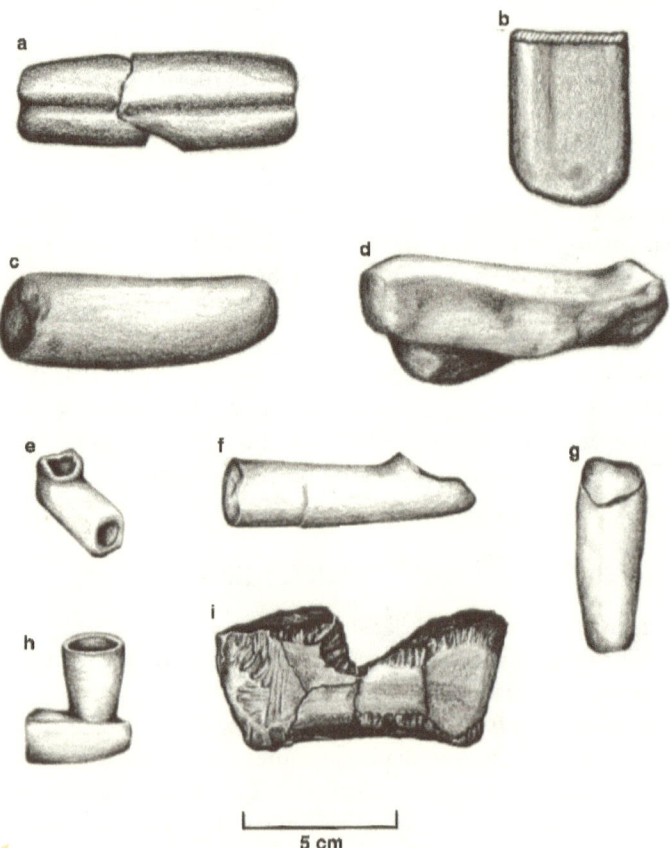

5 cm

ABRADERS

Abraders are ground stone artifacts of irregular form. As in the case of the bone specimens, this classification is only tentative. The criteria followed in assigning material to this type were taken from Carlson's (1973:71-2) abrader type.

Stone Abraders (Figure 12c). Eight specimens, four from each lodge, are classified abraders. All of these specimens exhibit smoothing on the majority of their surface areas. Some have been worn down to produce a rounded end. There is no identifiable pattern to their shapes. However, three of the four specimens from House 1 may be fragments of boat-shaped shaft smoothers. Also, three of the four specimens from House 2 have an oval or round cross-section and have been rounded on one end. One of the possible shaft smoother fragments from House 1 is made from Dakota sandstone; the remainders of the abraders are coarse-grained sandstone. The variations in measures for these specimens are as follows: Length - 104 to 56mm; Width - 54 to 33mm; Thickness - 36 to 23mm. Two fragments from House 1 are heavily impregnated with a red and a yellow material, probably hematite, which may indicate use in pigment processing. The three rounded specimens have been stained orangish-red - primarily along the rounded edges on the end. Such tools may have been used for smoothing in pottery manufacture. Carlson (1973:72) identified, tentatively, a piece similarly stained around the edge as a pottery-smoothing tool.

WHETSTONES

Wedel (1936:79-80) described "whetstones" as non-utilitarian objects primarily occurring in graves. The specimens herein reported and those examined by Carlson (1973:72) were for utilitarian purposes and were recovered from houses. Several of the specimens were used for at least two different functions.

Whetstones (Figure 12b). Four artifacts, three from House 1 and one from House 2, are classified whetstones. All are fragments. One specimen from House 1 is extremely well made from a piece of Ogallala quartzite. This specimen shows the least evidence of use of any of the examples. The other three are made from fine-grained sandstone (2 specimens) and an unidentified variety of quartzite. The quartzite specimen from House 2 and one of the sandstone specimens from House 1 have battered ends. The quartzite piece is impregnated with a yellow material (hematite) and the sandstone piece is impregnated with a red material (hematite). As is the case with other types of artifacts, these pieces too seem to have been used as pestles at least occasionally to produce some sort of mineral powder (paint?). All of the pieces have ovoid or rounded rectangular cross-sections.

One face has been worn very smooth and is either flat or slightly concave. The opposite face is slightly convex. The flat or concave surface would be the primary working surface.

Discussion. There is a significant finding at the Kansas Monument site in regard to the question of whether or not whetstones are ceremonial or utilitarian. Three of the four specimens occur in House 1, the house from which the majority of the iron knives were recovered. The two whetstone fragments that were not of possible ceremonial significance were recovered from the same excavation unit as the most complete knife (Figure 15e) from the site. Thus, there is at least this circumstantial evidence for the utilitarian aspect of whetstones.

PIPES

Stone pipes are the only kind known on Pawnee sites. The specimens from the Kansas Monument site support this as all are of stone. Two complete specimens differ morphologically, but are examples of the typical Pawnee elbow pipe.

Elbow Pipes (Figs. 12e-f, h-i). Two fairly complete elbow pipes were recovered from House 2 along with a pipe preform. The same combination was found in House 1. All of these artifacts are made from very fine-grained sandstone, orangish-red to gray in color. Specimen 14157 (Figure 12h) is almost completely intact. The stem is rectangular, tapers to form a keel projecting beyond the bowl, and has a length of 37mm. From the bottom of the stem to the top of the bowl it measures 39mm. The interior diameter of the bowl is 16mm, the outer diameter being 22mm. The stem has an interior diameter of 8mm and a maximum width of 17mm. The bowl wall has a thickness of 3mm and the stem wall has a thickness of 5mm. The other pipe lacks its bowl. It has a length of 35mm. The stem is almost round but has a flat bottom. The interior diameter of the stem is 9mm and the outer diameter is 17mm. The hole for the bowl tapers perfectly to a hole in the bottom of the pipe. This was probably an error during construction of the pipe. The stem wall has a thickness of 4mm.

Pipe Preforms (Figs. 12f and i). One pipe preform was recovered from each house. The preform from House 2 (Figure 12i) is for an elbow pipe similar to the one in Figure 12h. It has a length of 95mm. The highest point is on the portion from which the bowl will be shaped, 46mm. The maximum thickness of the piece is 29mm. Some rounding has already been performed on the specimen. The hole for the bowl has also been started. The piece shows definite cutting marks along the stem and on the bowl. It is suggested that the piece is too far into construction for the large mass to still be left on the stem unless the intent was to include this material in the subsequent modification. A preform such as this could be used to produce a pipe similar to one from the Hill site (see Wedel 1936, PI. 8, Figure Id).

The preform from House 1 (Figure 12f) is a pipe stem with a semi-lunar facet. Birkby (1962:13) suggests that the facet across the top of the piece is the result of the bowl breaking off. The stem is round with a maximum diameter of 23mm. From its widest point the piece tapers to a small keel beyond the semi-lunar facet, 81mm away. It should be noted that in the surface collections from the site are pipes made from similar red sandstone material as this piece but are covered with a slip.

Pipe Fragments. Fragments were recovered from both houses. Both pieces are sections of bowls. The determination that they came from the bowl area is based on the tapering thicknesses of the pieces. It is important to note that the fragment from House 1 has an attribute the House 2 specimen lacks, the base of the bowl is constricted and grooved. This characteristic can be seen on other pipes.

MISCELLANEOUS

Included in this category are the unidentified or unmodified pieces from the lithic assemblage. Artifacts are grouped by major categories under chipped and ground stone. Unmodified specimens are grouped by material such as hematite and other substances.

Petrified Wood. A rectangular piece of petrified wood was found in House 1. The piece has a length of 87mm, a width of 21mm and thickness of 11mm. This piece was originally classified a whetstone, but there is no evidence to indicate such a use. The only modification present is the rounding of the edges on one side and this is considered to be the result of natural processes.

Hematite. A quantity of red and yellow hematite (ochre) was recovered from each house. There is a problem in quantifying this material due to preservation inconsistencies. Any quantification using weight or count would be misleading. Therefore at this time it can be only recorded that both houses did have hematite present. It can also be noted that yellow ochre occurred only in House 2. Hematite that had not been powdered was recovered only from House 1. Most of the specimens of this red mineral have scars from scraping and grinding by the aboriginals.

Ground Stone (Figs. 12d and g). Five specimens of ground stone of unknown function were recovered. Two amorphous pieces of Dakota sandstone from House 2 have been partially ground but not enough to produce a level surface or a geometrically regular shape. The remainder of the unidentifiable specimens comes from House 1. One of these specimens is a round piece, oval in cross-section. It is of an unknown material, probably sandstone that has been very seriously altered by exposure to intense heat. This artifact shows some smoothing on one surface. It was apparently this smoothing combined with the unusually regular shape that lead to it being classified as a mano and an abrading stone at different times. Since there is no evidence to suggest that the form is not the product of natural forces and the wear on the one surface is slight, this piece can only be considered a ground stone of unknown function.

A second specimen from House 1 (Figure 12g) is a small piece of very fine-grained gray sandstone. This artifact is only 62mm long, 22mm wide at its widest, and 12mm thick. It has been ground smooth on all surfaces. The narrow end of the piece has been ground almost round. The wider end is almost flat. The flaring of the sides from narrow end to wide end is very gradual. This piece may have been a pendant but it lacks the scoring usually associated with such pieces. There is red staining around the narrow end and extending about one third to one half the distance down the piece. This staining may be indicative of the piece being used in pottery making.

The fourth unidentified ground stone piece from House 1 (Figure 12d) was originally classified an abrader. This specimen is 100mm long and has been flattened on both ends. From the narrow end, 41mm wide, the sides gently flare out to a width of 49mm, 51mm down the length of the piece. At that point the sides abruptly expand to a width of 56mm in just a few millimeters distance and then continue to expand to a terminal width of 62mm. The ground surface of the piece slopes from the narrow end until it reaches the point where the sides expand. At that point the ground surface levels off abruptly. The net result of these attributes is that the piece when viewed in profile looks like a ski jump ramp. Why this artifact was modified in such a manner is unknown. The function of a piece of this form is unknown. No similar specimens have been observed in the literature.

Flakes and Chips (Figure 9f). Flakes and chips were recovered from both houses and the disturbed grave. Again there is the problem of quantification since not all specimens were saved. Thus, all that can be done is to note the presence of these artifacts. There are several pieces that merit attention. A large flake of red chert (alibates ?) from House 1 was used as a scraper and was modified for use as a graver. A flake of chert from the Florence formation recovered from House 2 was also used as a scraper and graver. The final piece that merits mention is a scraper made from the base of a broken projectile point (Figure 9f). The point was made from translucent quartzite, had a concave base, and was notched. This specimen is 32mm wide across the base. This base is almost identical to the base of a complete specimen made from translucent white quartzite recovered from a grave at the Hill site (Wedel 1936:75). The Kansas Monument site specimen is from House 2.

Ground Stone Fragments. Thirteen fragments of ground stone were recovered in the excavations, all from House 2 with the exception of a Dakota quartzite fragment from House 1. The material from House 2 is comprised of three pieces of Ogallala quartzite, two pieces of sandstone, and seven pieces of Dakota quartzite. The Dakota quartzite specimens were recovered together and are probably from the same original implement. Only one of the fragments is sufficiently large to allow any statement in regards to the type of tool it came from. One of the Ogallala quartzite fragments from House 2 has a surface that has been carefully smoothed and indicates it was concave. This may be a fragment of a stone mortar such as that recovered from House 1. The fragment suggests this, but there is too little evidence to be conclusive.

Rough Stone. A large piece of yellow hematite was recovered from House 2. The small concavities present on two surfaces are the result of some natural process. Since this piece is not demonstrably modified or used in any way by man, it is designated as rough stone. The ultimate purpose of its presence at the site may have been to produce yellow ochre.

DISCUSSION

The most interesting aspect of the lithic assemblage from the Kansas Monument site is not the quantity of material but the composition. The majority of the traditional tools present are those used by women: scrapers, mortars, and abraders. The only tools normally associated with a strictly male activity are the shaft smoothers. Metal counterparts have replaced all projectile points, knives, and axes; tools commonly used by males in their usual behavioral roles. Therefore, it is fair to say that trade with Euro-Americans made a direct and considerable impact on male Pawnee behavior from the very beginning. The females, from the material culture standpoint, were little affected, continuing on in traditional behaviors with traditional tools. This is a situation that has been noted in the ethnological literature many times.

BONE ARTIFACTS

It is unfortunate, but many of the bones, including the bone tools, have continued to deteriorate since they were recovered. Fortunately, an early study of the bone material (Birkby 1962) is available. The data contained in that study helped to fill in the gaps caused by deterioration of the material.

Scapula Hoes (Figure 13a). A total of eight whole or fragmentary scapula hoes were recovered. The only specimen sufficiently complete to be measured has an overall length of 440mm and a maximum blade length of 161mm. The articular butts of five of the hoes had been removed. None of the specimens retain their spinous processes. Additional modification of the hoes was accomplished by cutting along the caudal- and cephalic-borders. The seven hoes recovered from the bottom of Feature 1 show wear along the vertebral border, indicating use as implements (Birkby

1962:14). The single specimen recovered from Feature 3 was too fragmentary to retain any evidence of use.

Figure 13. Bone Artifacts: a. Scapula Hoe; b. Boneflesher; c. Elk Antler Scraper.

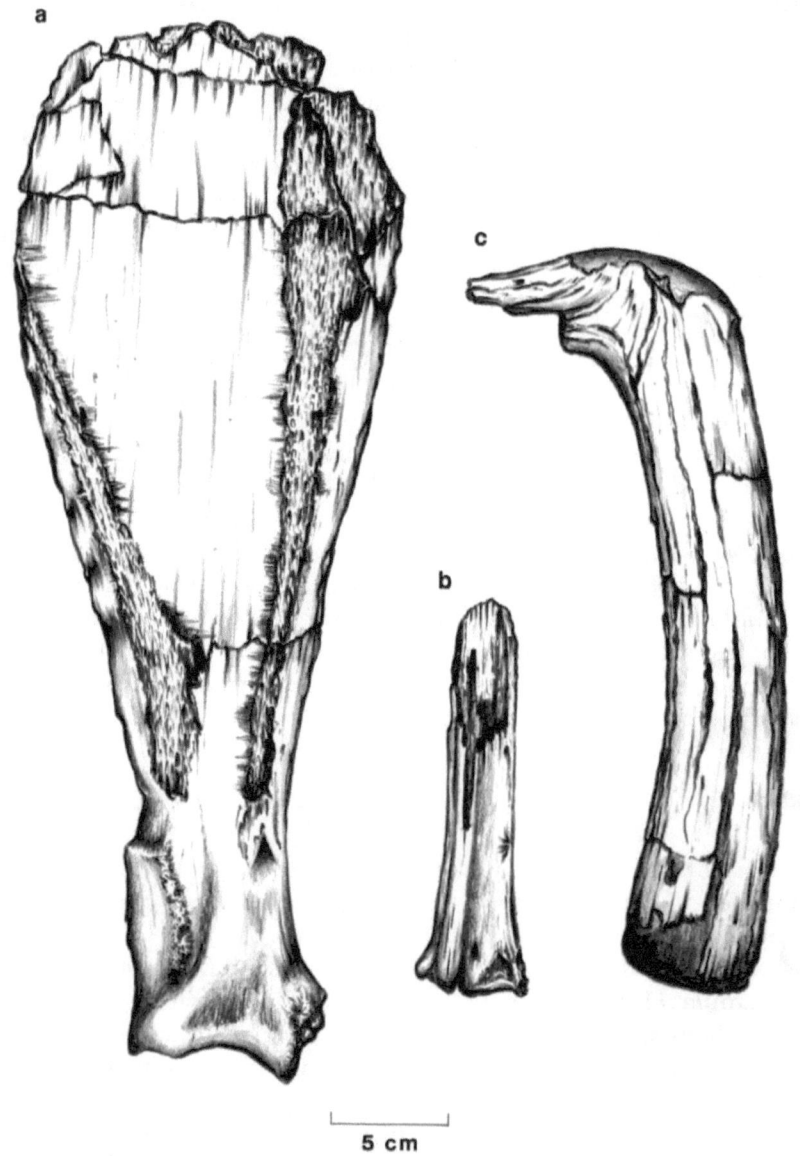

5 cm

Boneflesher (Figure 13b). A single specimen was recovered from the midden area, Feature 7, north of House 2. Made from the proximal end of a bison metatarsal, the piece has an overall length of 167mm and a width of 45mm at the joint and 23mm at the working end. Although part of the working edge is missing, enough remains to identify the notching which is common on fleshers from late sites (Wedel 1936:84). The joint forms the butt of the piece and the working edge is rounded.

Shaft Wrench. A group of charred bone fragments was identified as a shaft wrench (Birkby 1962:15). This single specimen was recovered from Feature 3. The wrench appears to have been fashioned from a bison rib. The fragmentary nature of the artifact precluded any measurements.

Elk Antler Scrapers (Figure 13c). Three elk antler scrapers were recovered, two from House 2 and one from House 1. Two of the specimens were repaired and restored using plaster of Paris. The larger reconstructed specimen measures 325mm in length and has a mid-shaft diameter of 52mm. The occurrence of one of the specimens with a possible seed corn cache, previously mentioned, suggests that these tools may have had a role in planting as well as being used in hide preparation.

Abraders. Two pieces of cancellous bone were identified by the flat, worn, and smooth surfaces of the cancellous sections. However, there is no evidence of wear or polishing on the articular surfaces.

Cut Antler. House 2 produced a single cut piece of antler. The overall length of the piece is 291mm. There is evidence of wear on the tip of the specimen, but its function is unknown.

Miscellaneous Bone. Not all of the recovered bone material was kept for analysis. All that can be presented is an identification of the species present. Indications as to what predominated are taken from the field notes. The largest number of bones is attributed to bison (*Bison bison*). There were also some deer (*Odocoileus*), wapiti (*Cervidae*), bear (*Ursidae*), and dog, coyote, or wolf (*Canidae*) present. Also present was beaver (*Castor Canadensis*). In addition, fresh water mussel shells, bird bones, and reptilian bones are present.

Discussion. There is nothing in the bone tool assemblage to suggest any major change or deviation from Pawnee tool assemblages. The presence of these tools instead suggests that at the time the site was inhabited, the Pawnee were still producing some traditional goods and were not yet fully dependent on Euro-American sources for raw materials and tools. Considering the fact that tools of European manufacture or made from European materials that could take the place of the traditional bone tools are present, the evidence suggests that contact was not of sufficient length or steady enough to produce the dependency that marks the Pawnee of later historic times.

WOODEN ARTIFACTS

In an area such as the Central Plains, it is unusual for wood to survive for any great length of time once it has been deposited in the ground. Therefore, it is not surprising that wooden artifacts comprise the smallest of the material categories present.

Wooden Mortar. One example of a wooden mortar was recovered from House 2 where it had been imbedded in the floor. The piece is currently a bag of rubble with no fragments greater than an inch in diameter. Unfortunately, no notes have turned up which record any of the dimensions or condition of the mortar when it was found. Its present state precludes any statements along this line. Wooden mortars were not uncommon on Pawnee sites according to historical accounts (see Irving 1835; also Wedel 1936:88). They were fashioned by burning out a block of wood. Primarily they were used to grind corn. Wedel (1936:88) states that wooden mortars were used in place of stone metates. This may be the case since the only metate recovered at the site was not from House 2. There are pieces of ground stone present in House 2 that may be from stone metates or mortars but these pieces are too fragmentary for identification.

METAL ARTIFACTS

Artifacts made from metal form one of the largest categories at the Kansas Monument site. Given the chemical nature of most metals, much of this material is in very poor condition hampering classification. All metal artifacts are Euro-American in origin, but the natives for other uses have modified some. The artifacts have been sorted along functional lines, using the original Euro-American function whenever possible.

HOES

Three iron hoes were recovered during the University of Kansas excavation. Each of these is morphologically distinguishable from the others on the basis of blade shape. All three of the specimens were recovered from House 2.

Hoop-Skirt Blade (Figure 14a). The single recovered specimen is badly rusted. It has an overall length of 188mm, a socket height of 44mm, a maximum blade width of 155mm, and a thickness of 9mm at the eye and 3mm at the working edge. A short neck is present where the blade was melded to the socket. No marker's marks are discernible. This piece is similar to an identified French specimen from the Longest site (A.D. 1750-1800) in Oklahoma (Bell et al. 1967, Figure 48b). This variety of hoe is called "hoop-skirt" because the blade has a very distinctive shape, reminiscent of a hoop-skirt in profile.

Figure 14. Iron Hoes: a. Hoop-Skirt Blade; b. Pear Blade; c. Round Blade.

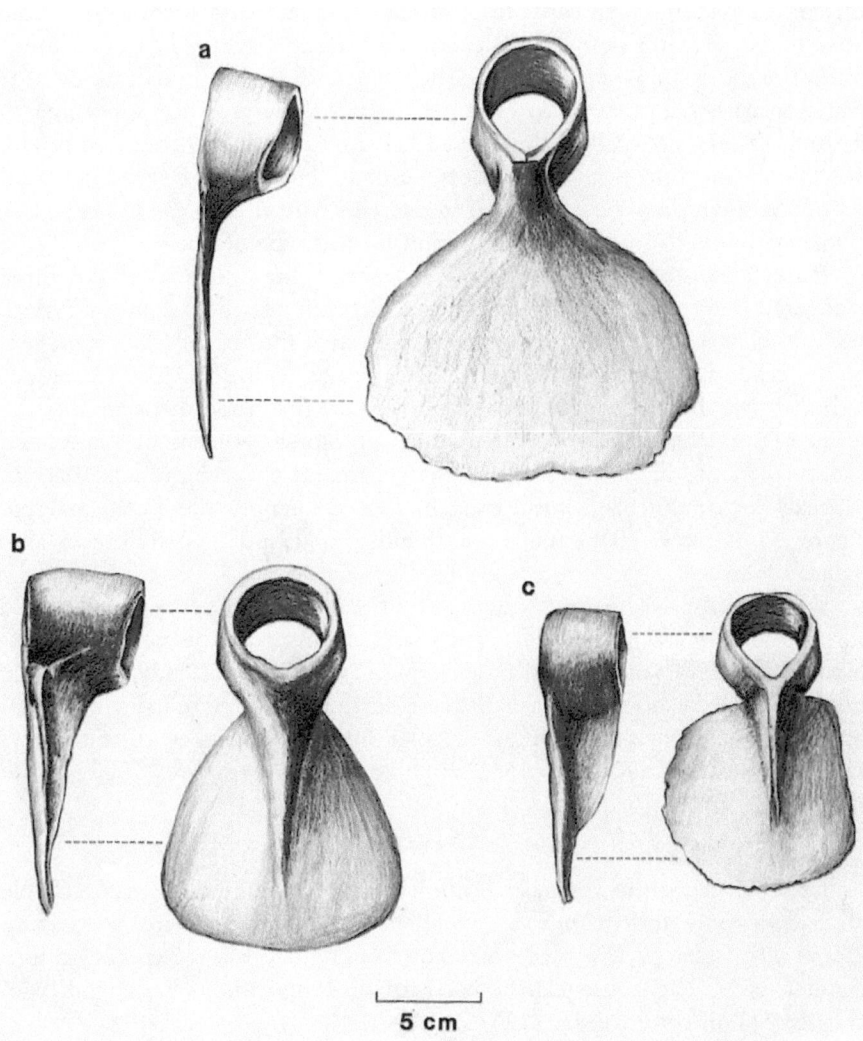

5 cm

Pear Blade (Figure 14b). This single specimen is small but massive in proportions. Its overall length is 163mm, its socket height is 57mm, its maximum blade width is 114mm, and the thickness of the metal varies from 10mm at the eye to 5mm on the working edge. Of all the recovered specimens, this one has the widest socket and the thickest blade, socket wall, and ridge. There is no neck. A ridge tapers from the socket down approximately 4/5 of the blade's median. The bottom edge is beveled, possibly from use. The shoulders slope off abruptly from the eye, producing the distinctive pear shape of the blade. This piece is the product of hand forging, but no maker's marks are visible. Russell (1967: 342-4, Figure 84g) illustrates and describes an almost identical specimen from a Wisconsin Menomini Indian site of unknown date. Russell considers these hoes to be an early type of trade hoe of French origin. Two specimens from the Fort St. Joseph site in Michigan and the Fatherland site near Natchez, Mississippi, are also examples of this variety of hoe according to Russell. These sites fall in the 1700-1760 time range. It should be noted, however, that hoes of this variety, called "Hoes for Brush" are still produced today for sale in Latin America (see Russell 1967:342, 344). The evidence points to an early French origin for this type of hoe.

Round Blade (Figure 14c). This piece is the smallest of the three recovered hoes, being only 140mm in length, with a socket height of 39mm, and a thickness of 4mm on the blade and 9mm at the socket. The right side of the blade is missing, precluding measures of width, but the remainder indicates that the blade was almost round. Since this blade shape may be the result of use, this type is only tentative. No similar specimens have been observed in the literature. A ridge that begins at the eye gradually slopes medially down the blade until over half of the length has been covered. There is no neck. The piece was hand-forged and has no perceivable maker's marks.

Discussion. The distinctiveness of the three hoes just discussed suggests that with further data, such implements may be very useful in establishing trade sources and time periods. Comparisons indicate that the hoop-skirt-blade hoes and the pear-blade hoes may both be of French origin and occur in sites dating *ca.* 1750-1760. These data seem to support an early date for the Kansas Monument site.

KNIVES

Excavations at the Kansas Monument site produced four recognizable knife fragments and no whole specimens. All four fragments were from House 1. Three of the pieces are large enough to allow separation into distinct types. The nomenclature used for these specimens is derived from Haggerty (1963) and Russell (1967:213).

Sheepfoot Point (Figure 15c). One of the fragments has been identified as a sheepfoot-point case knife. These knives are so called because of the characteristic curved back with a convex edge forming a blade shaped like a sheep's foot. Such knives were "favored by some Indian artisans for scribing, perforating, mortising, and carving wood and stiff rawhide" (Russell 1967:209). This specimen has a forward sloping heel. A wooden or bone handle was attached to the blade by pins passing through the holes in the flat handle. The width is 25mm at the heel and 12mm on the handle. The specimen is pitted with rust but there is no evidence of any sort of maker's mark.

Figure 15. Trade Axes and Knives: a. Large Axe; b. Small Axe; c. Sheepfoot Point Knife; d. Bowed-Back Knife; e. Bellied Edge Knife; f. Large Knife (Sword?) Fragment.

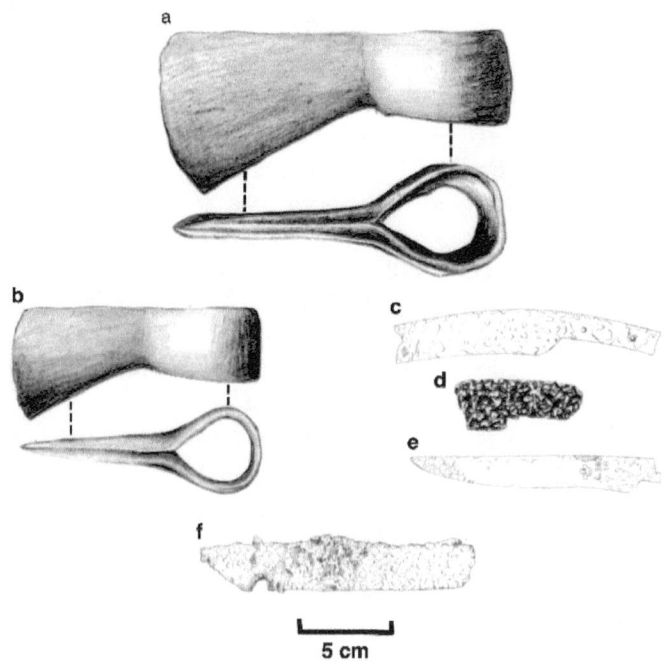

5 cm

Bowed-Back Blade (Figure 15d).   Another case knife specimen recovered from House 1 also had a bowed back. The angle formed by the arc of the back is smaller than that for the sheepfoot point. This specimen is also much larger proportionately than that characterized above. The fragment has a width 28mm at its short, straight heel. The flat handle has a width of 20mm. There is no evidence of holes in the tang for attachment of a handle. The thickness of the tang tapers from approximately 4mm where it is joined with the heel, to approximately 1mm at the proximal end. On the basis of this, it is surmised that the tang is more or less complete. No similar specimens have been observed in the literature.

Bellied Edge Blade (Fig 15e). A case knife specimen from House 1 is distinct from the other fragments because of its bellied edge. This fragment has a straight back and a slightly forward jutting heel. The blade is whole and has a length of 123.5mm. The piece was broken at the first hole in the tang. Smith recovered similar specimens during a surface collection at the site. A maker's mark is visible on the blade. The mark is a crown with three points, each point ending in a *fleur de lis*, resembling the symbol of the St. Etienne armory. Beneath the crown is the inscription, C.IA / -IS. None of the recovered specimens have similar marks, nor has this mark been recorded at any of the sites used in this report for comparison. This piece has a width of 18mm at the heel and 11mm on the tang.

Fragments. A fragment from House 1 may be the distal tip of a blade. It is too incomplete to be grouped in any of the above types. The classification of the piece as a knife fragment is based entirely on its cross-section, which is triangular. A poorly preserved fragment of a large, probably steel knife blade (Figure 15f) was recovered from House 2. The specimen was identified as a knife fragment because of its cross-section and size. The piece is obviously larger than any of the knives recovered from the site. The cross-section, though triangular like that of a knife, shows that the blade edge was rounded on the end where the blade was widest. This condition is characteristic of sword blades of many varieties that the author has observed in many collections. The cross-section of the fragment also shows that the piece tapers in both width and thickness of blade. The condition of the specimen precludes the identification of any maker's marks. It can be stated with certainty that this blade had neither a bezel (sloping face) nor a fuller (groove). This piece may be from the proximal end of a sword that was not very long and was of low quality.

Discussion. It is interesting to note that all of the specimens, with the exception of one fragment, come from House 1 and that all are case knives. There were no specimens of the popular clasp knife recovered during excavation, although one is present in the Nystrum collection. These data again indicate that there may have been a distinct difference between the inhabitants of House 1 and House 2. There may have been a differential involvement in the trade business of this time.

TRADE AXES

Two complete axes and one axe fragment were recovered in the excavations. These axes are of the variety called camp or belt axes (Woodward 1946:6, Figure 3). These were common throughout the 18th Century and comprise axes smaller than those originally introduced into the Indian trade. The small size made it useful for both light wood chopping and warfare. In addition, these specimens are also referred to as half axes or half hatchets (Peterson 1965:6). This designation refers to the fact that rather than the double flaring blade that was common on the earliest forms of trade axes, only the edge toward the hand flared. The leading edge was straight or slightly convex.

All of the specimens are hand forged. The two complete specimens were made without the imbedded steel edge common among the better trade axes. Although similar in form, the two complete axes are distinguishable on the basis of size. Woodward (1946, Figure 3) shows a collection of trade axes of varying sizes gathered at Fort Ticonderoga. Size may be useful in distinguishing period of manufacture and, possibly, place of origin. It appears, however, from the data at hand that size may be characteristic of the individual smith who made the axe. When European firms on a mass scale produced trade axes, size and form seems to have been fairly standardized, but when local blacksmiths were responsible for trade axe production, these variables become less diagnostic. As more data become available, it may be possible to say more about the importance of size and shape in trade axes.

Large Axe (Figure 15a). This iron specimen from House 2 has an overall length of 192mm. The working edge is 89mm long. The eye has a diameter of 50mm. There is no steel edge. Folding the sheet iron short of the edge, welding the piece together, formed the blade. The superior line of the axe is straight; the inferior line is concave. This axe has an eye that is almost round. Morphologically, this axe resembles a specimen from the Fatherland site, 1682-1729 (Neitzel 1965, Pl. 14 x), and one from the Guebert site (1719-1813) (Good 1972, Figure 38d; Figure 39d). There is no poll on this axe but there is flattening at the back of the eye. Such flattening indicates that the axe may have been used as a hammer or wedge.

The single axe fragment, also from House 2, is the eye and small portion of the blade. It was probably from an axe similar to the large axe described and also shows flattening at the rear of the eye.

Small Axe (Figure 15b). This small piece from House 1 has an overall length of 133mm. It has an almost round eye with a diameter of 40mm. The convex working edge is 60mm long. The method of fabrication was similar to that of the large axe. The superior line is slightly convex with a quick sloping off at the leading edge. The inferior line of the blade is concave. This form is reminiscent of the Type C trade axe defined by Bouchard (1976:18). Type C trade axes were in Canada after 1760. There are no maker's marks.

Discussion. Considering the amount of variability in trade axes it is difficult to be specific about these specimens. They are undoubtedly of French manufacture. Temporally they could be placed anywhere in the 18th Century. The smaller axe may be post 1760, if it is a Canadian axe.

GUN PARTS

In terms of identifiable specimens, gun parts comprise the largest single category of trade goods. The only missing gun parts are ramrod pipes, trigger plates, front sites, sears, and various screws and pins. No wooden parts of trade guns were recovered.

Flintlock Mechanism (Figure 16a). A nearly complete flintlock mechanism was recovered from House 1. The following is Smith's original description of the piece:

Figure 16. Gun Parts: a. Flintlock Mechanism; b. Cock; c. Barrel Pin Lug; d. Trigger Guard Fragment; e. Serpentine Sideplate Fragment; f. Rear Gun Site; g. Low Relief Sideplate.

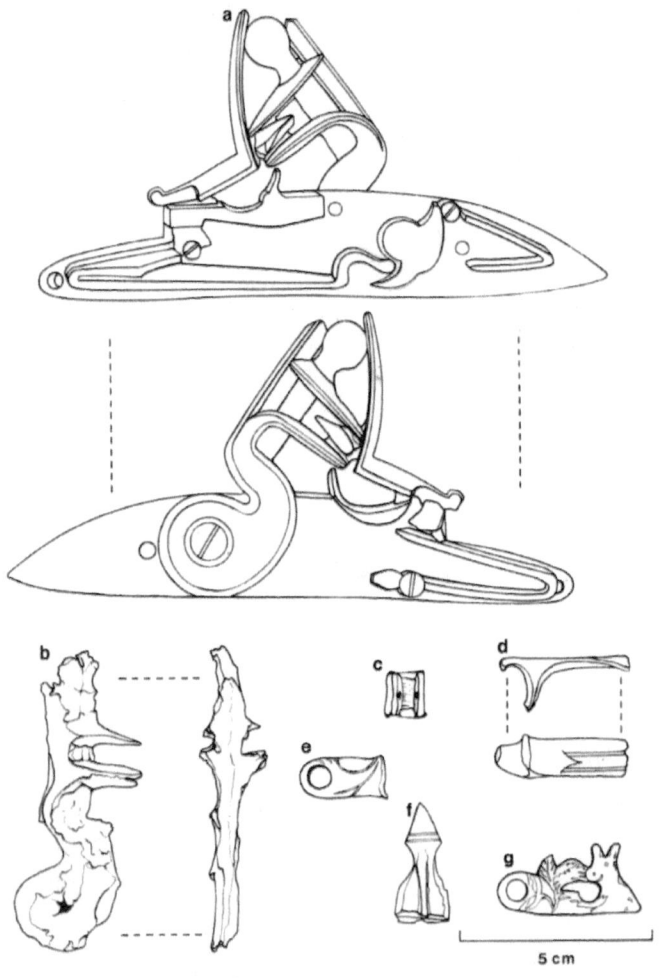

The lock resembles those found on French military muskets of the Models 1728 and 1746, manufactured until 1754 (Hicks 1936:13, 36). The lock plate terminates in a point to the rear of the hammer and is rounded at the forward end. There is no groove behind the hammer. It is equipped with a removable pan having a fence and was made without the conventional tenon for the support of the frizzen screw. The frizzen is round at the top, has a low median ridge, and is equipped with a curled spur at its forward extremity. The frizzen spring has a finial in the shape of a laurel leaf. The hammer, or cock, is of the gooseneck variety, flat with a beveled edge. A screw secures the cap with a perforated and notched head in the form of a sphere. The posterior edge of the cap has a rectangular notch that slides on the spur of the hammer. A gunflint is held in the jaws of the hammer. An engraved line borders the plate and the hammer. The interior mechanism is of conventional construction except for the tumbler that has a thin spur at the rear formed by removing metal from under the surface. Furthermore, no provision is made for a bridle. The other parts consist of the mainspring and sear spring. The sear is missing. (Smith 1950a: 4)

The lock plate is flat and has a length of 146mm. The maximum width of the plate is 26mm. Measuring from the top of the comb to the base of the cock's body, a standard measure in gun literature, the length is 76mm. A second standard measure is the "throw," from the lip of the lower vise jaw of the cock to the midpoint of the screw hole on the cock body, this is 40mm.

Little is known about the 18th Century French trade gun. Harris, et al. (1965) and Hamilton (1968) gathered together sufficient amounts of data to make some pertinent statements about the form of these guns. This information is directly applicable to the flintlock mechanism just described.

Hayward (1963:49, 200; as noted in Harris, et al. 1965:320) reports that cocks with flat faces on flat locks were characteristic of French arms from the late 17th Century to the mid-18th Century. British trade guns from this period until *ca.* 1875 had rounded faces behind the cock and on the body of the cock (Harris et al. 1965:321). Therefore, the evidence is that this lock is from a French gun (its size suggests a fowling piece or light musket) possibly manufactured between 1700 and 1750, *if* it is a reasonably high quality piece. Pieces made expressly for the fur trade often retain characteristics of early fine guns for long periods of time. It should be noted that this lock is similar to the pieces from the Gilbert site (Jelks 1967, Figs. 32 and 33). Thus, the early date (*ca.* 1750) may not be out of line for this lock.

Additional data for the controversy on French gun parts is presented by the flashpan. The absence of a tenon to support the frizzen is common on quality French arms made prior to the middle of the 18th Century (Harris et al. 1965: 321) but continued on trade guns long after then as an economy measure. Thus, it is hard to be specific about this piece. It is the author's belief that this lock can tentatively be considered a French trade gun, possibly of above average quality (chief's grade?), manufactured *ca.* 1750.

Cock (Figure 16b). House 1 also produced a flintlock cock that was not attached to its lock. From the top of the comb to the bottom of the body is a measure of 68mm. From the lip of the lower vise jaw to the approximated mid-point of the screw hole is a measure of 38mm. The piece is in bad condition due to continuing oxidation. This may result in a small error being involved with the above measures. There are sufficient amounts of detail left to indicate that this cock was also of the flat face variety with a beveled edge. This piece is also of the gooseneck variety, however, the angle of the neck is not nearly as sharp as that of the other cock. A principle difference between this cock and the other is the comb. The comb on this specimen is wide, forming a laurel leaf from the lower vise jaw. Additionally, there is a medial ridge running the length of the comb. The vise screw is present but it is too corroded to preserve its original form. It possibly was bulbous, perforated, and had a niche on the top like the specimen on the complete lock.

There are similarities and differences between the two cocks in the collection. The single cock is undoubtedly from a smaller piece. The wide comb is identical to the combs on the locks illustrated in Harris et al. (1965, Figure 11) and Jelks (1967, Figs. 32-4). This, combined with its flat face and beveled edge, indicates that there is no reason that it too could not be from the same time period.

Wide combs such as that on the smaller cock were common on guns of the early and middle 18th Century. The narrow comb became predominant in the early 19th Century. The two styles overlapped during the latter part of the 18th Century. Thus, the presence of both styles in a single house suggests a time period in the 18th Century. This agrees with the earlier date for the site.

Frizzen. A single frizzen was recovered from House 1. It is broken above the point where it was joined to the pan cover, so it is impossible to determine its height. A width of 23mm compares favorably with a width of 24mm for the frizzen on the complete lock. There is also a slight curvature of the piece but this is not as pronounced as in the other frizzen. This piece may be the frizzen from the smaller gun represented by the cock that was previously described. However, the dimensional differences are not so great as to prevent this piece from having been on a lock similar to that found.

Flashpan (Figure 17f). A removable flashpan was recovered from House 1. This iron piece was attached to the lock by a screw passed through its interior tang. It has a shallow trough with a low flash shield at its rear. On a line parallel to the flash shield, the piece measures 24mm. On a line perpendicular to the flash shield, it measures 22mm. The distal portion of the tang is missing. This piece conforms in all identifiable attributes with the pan on the complete lock.

Figure 17. Gun Parts: a. Gun Barrel Tent Peg; b. Buttplate Fragment; c. Gun Barrel Hammer; d. Side Plate Screw; e. Sear Spring; f. Flashpan; g. Gun Barrel Scraper

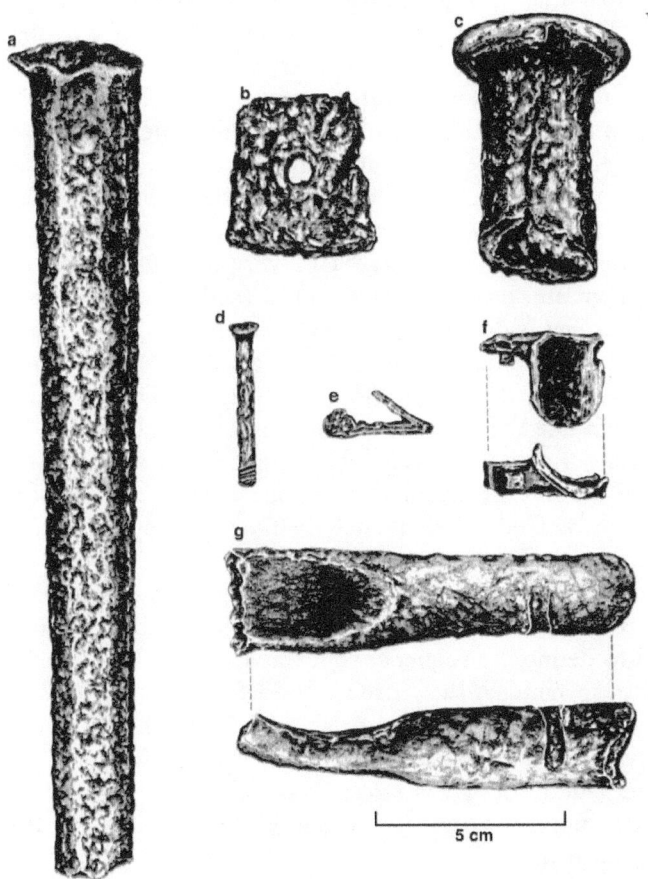

5 cm

Sear Spring (Figure 17e). Among the additional gun parts recovered from House 1 is a complete sear spring. From the screw hole to the bend, the piece measures 29mm. From the bend to the end that operates the sear measures 18mm. This sear spring is much smaller than the one on the complete lock. This specimen may have been on the lock with the small hammer, previously described.

Mainspring. House 2 produced one definite and one possible mainspring fragment. The definite specimen is the upper leaf of the mainspring having broken at the bend. The small portion of the mainspring that extends beyond the screw mount is also missing. The remnant of the stud that fits in a perforation on the lock is visible on the interior edge. The piece is in too poor condition to warrant measurements, but a comparison between it and the mainspring on the complete lock reveals that this artifact is much larger in every dimension.

A possible mainspring fragment was recovered from the center of House 2. This fragment represents the upper leaf of a V-shaped spring. The stud is clearly visible on the interior edge. There is evidence that removing the screw mount and shaping the remaining end to a point purposefully modified this piece. Possibly the intent was to prepare the piece for use as a projectile point. This piece would have been used on a much smaller lock than the complete specimen. It should be noted that although the piece is classified as a mainspring, it could be a frizzen spring.

Sideplates (Figs. 16e and g). Two very different forms of sideplates, one a fragment and one whole, were unearthed. The fragment is the distal end of a serpent side-plate, recovered from House 2. Visible on the fragment are the feathers from the head of the dragon. The feathers are delicately executed in a piece of flat cast brass. The end of the piece is serrated much like the edge of the modern American dime. The sides of the piece are serrated diagonally, upper right to lower left. The hole has a diameter of 5mm. An examination of the broken edge indicates that the piece was cut or filed approximately half way through then folded until it could be broken off.

There is a transition involved with serpentine sideplates, but the sequence is little understood. Hamilton (1968) and Hanson (1956) have attempted to define the sequence, but this fragment is too small to place it among the specimens they used. Bouchard (1976:104) suggests that sideplates executed in the manner above date *ca.* 1750. Such a position would tally with the dates for the other gun parts. It should also be noted that the serpentine design is strongly associated with English trade guns. This in turn suggests post 1767, which is the date that the British gained control of the area.

From House 1 comes another fragment of brass side-plate. It has a length of 36mm, a width of 18mm and a thickness of 2mm. There is a screw hole with a diameter of 5mm. The decoration is a low relief casting of an animal, possibly a deer or a dog, and a leafy plant. Casting in low relief became popular on French trade guns during the 1770's (Blaine and Harris 1967:70-1). Though it cannot be stated with any certainty, such a chronological position would not be out of line with the data from the other gun parts. Smith suggests this fragment is from a Type B or C sideplate (Hamilton 1968: 3-7). French gunsmiths from 1680-1730 produced such sideplates.

Trigger Guard (Figure 16d). Another gun part from House 1 is a fragment of a brass trigger guard. The fragment is from the forward end of the bow guard and tang. On the tang is the latter part of an engraved scrollwork design. No similar pieces have been identified in the literature.

Rear Sight (Figure 16f). A brass rear sight was recovered from House 2. The sight has a pointed lozenge-shaped finial, and is engraved with two parallel lines directly above the widest point. The point of the finial is off center from the line of sight. The piece has an overall length of 31mm. The finial has a maximum width of 9mm and the body of the sight has a width of 14mm. A thickness, or height, of 8mm was recorded for the body and 1mm for the finial. This is an example of a Type C rear site (Hamilton 1968, Figure 5H). French gunsmiths from 1685-1730 produced type C trade guns.

Barrel Pin Lug (Figure 16c). One barrel pin lug was recovered from House 1. This iron lug would have been dovetailed into the underside of the barrel. Iron pins would have been passed through the hole and through the wood of the stock to secure the barrel. This specimen is 12mm long and 10mm wide. An identical specimen is illustrated in Jelks (1967, Figure 35e). This cannot be considered significant, however, as there is nothing to indicate that barrel pin lugs changed in any diagnostic fashion through time, but this correlates with the absence of barrel bands.

Butt Plate (Figure 17b). A fragment of an iron butt plate was unearthed in House 2. This fragment is from the heel of a flat plate. Flat plates are typical of trade guns. The hole is present through which one of the screws would have been passed to secure the butt plate to the stock. The plate was broken so that the screw hole is at the virtual center of the fragment. Possibly this piece was used as an ornament subsequent to its removal from the gun. The piece is too poorly preserved to ascertain whether it could have been used as a scraper or other tool.

Gun Barrels (Figure 17a, c, g). Four gun barrel fragments were found: Two in House 1, one in House 2, and one in the midden area behind Feature 7. All of these specimens were modified after being removed from their stocks. Both specimens from House 1 have been hammered on the breech end and lack tangs. This suggests use as tent pegs. Additionally, the longer specimen has been flattened out on the muzzle end and shows evidence of having been used for scraping or some other activity that would wear down the metal. Gun barrel fleshers copied from bone fleshers are not unknown in the Plains, but are usually notched.

The fragment from House 2 has been hammered into a mushroom shaped piece (Figure 17c). There are two notches on opposite sides of the barrel showing how the piece was split banana peel fashion as the top was hammered down. The octagonal shape of the barrel is only barely discernible, indicating heavy use. Also present is evidence of heavy battering on the head. These attributes suggest that the piece was used as a hammer.

The fragment from the midden area is from the rounded muzzle end of the barrel. This piece is open on its widest end and pounded flat on the muzzle end. The flattened end has been worn down; suggesting that this piece may have been used as a scraper or similar tool, as was suggested for one of the fragments from House 1.

From these pieces it is possible to make some statements about the original barrels present. The composite barrel indicated by these fragments was a smooth bore. It had an octagonal breech and a rounded muzzle. The length of the barrel was probably between 20 and 30 inches. The caliber has been estimated at between .55 and .69 (Smith 1950a: 4); .66 was the most common caliber for trade guns (Russell 1957:104).

Side Screw. One round-headed flintlock side screw was recovered from House 2. This piece is heavily encrusted with organic matter. The cap has a diameter of 13mm and the overall length of the piece is 47mm. It appears to be the equivalent of the modern 3/8 x 1.75 inch cap screw. The number of turns per unit of measure is impossible to estimate. Screws such as this were used to secure locks to the stock, passing through side plates.

Butt Plate Screw (Figure 17d). One flat-headed iron butt plate screw was recovered from House 1. Overall, the length is 44mm. The cap has a width of 8mm. This screw appears to be the equivalent of the modern 3/8 x 1.5 wood screw. There are 14 turns per 10mm. Flat-headed screws such as this were used to secure butt plates to stocks.

Discussion. The gunflints are included in the chipped stone section. What can be concluded from the metal parts is pertinent to the understanding of the site. From the brass fittings, it is possible to conclude that an above average quality gun was present. Most of these parts were associated with House 1. Noting the other differences between the houses mentioned in their discussion, the presence of these superior quality parts indicates that the inhabitants of House 1 were of high status. Possibly this was a chief's house.

Also, it can be concluded from the gun parts that they represent examples of guns manufactured by the French *ca.* 1750 to 1770. The presence of at least one English gun can be inferred from the dragon side plate. Additionally, certain of the smaller parts show distinct similarities with French guns produced early in the 18th and late in the 17th Century.

Thus, at this point status differences between the houses can be inferred and the evidence primarily suggests an occupation of the site during the third quarter of the 18th Century. The indicated date is particularly significant, as it agrees with the early dates assigned to the site (Wedel

1936:33) but disagrees substantially with the date indicated by Grange's (1968) seriation study.

METAL PROJECTILE POINTS

A total of nine whole, or nearly whole, projectile points were recovered in the excavations (Figure 18a-h). Also recovered were two large fragments and some small pieces that may be metal point fragments. The recovered specimens were divided into five types on the basis of morphology. Following Stone's (1974) example, these types can be further broken down by material of manufacture.

Figure 18 . Metal Projectile Points, Ornaments and a Nail: a. Basal Notched; b. triangular; c. & d. Stemmed Up-Turned Shoulders; e. Stemmed Triangular; f. & h. Lozenge Shaped; i. Lead Wire Ring; j. Copper trinket; k. Rosehead Nail; l. Iron Bracelet.

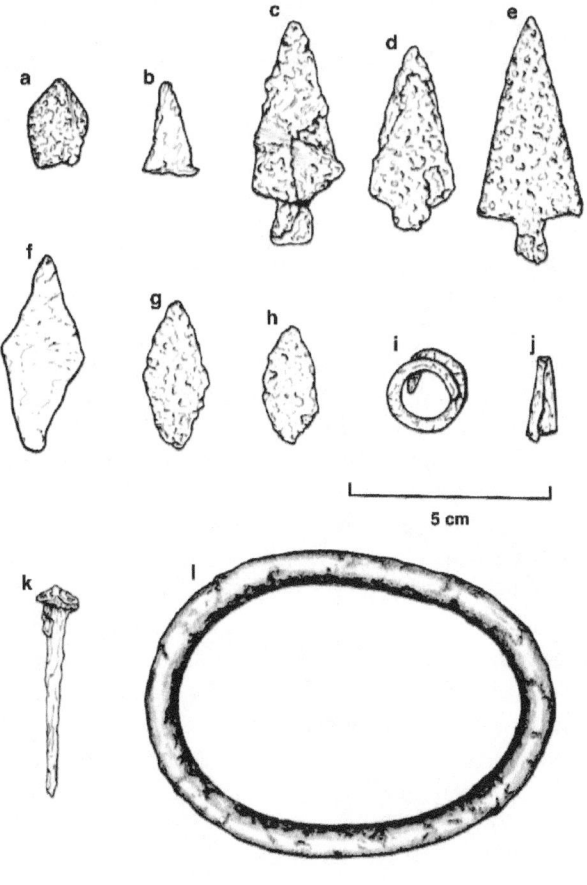

5 cm

Specimens occurred only within houses. Since no stone projectile points were discovered in the excavations, it appears that at the time when these two houses were inhabited, the Pawnee had abandoned the production of stone points in favor of the lighter and, in some cases, more durable metal points. Most of the points are undoubtedly of European origin but some, particularly the copper specimens, are crudely produced probably indicating an aboriginal origin. In many cases traders produced trade points by cutting them from rolled iron or hoops (Bradbury 1819:174-75). Smith recovered evidence that points were being manufactured from copper in House 1.

Basal Notched (Figure 18a). One specimen of this type was recovered from House 1. The point has a length of 22mm, a maximum width of 15mm, and a thickness of 3mm. This point is recognizable by its shape that resembles a lozenge that has been elongated then cut flat and notched on its base. Examples of similar points were found at Rosebough Lake, Texas (41BW5), 1719-1778 (Miroir, et al. 1973:144, Figure 11o), and the Gilbert site (41RA13), *ca.* 1750-1775, (Harris, et al. 1967:31, Figure 25e). All specimens are iron and, based on the Kansas example, it is doubtful that they are of aboriginal fabrication.

Triangular (Figure 18b). Two roughly triangular pieces of copper have been termed projectile points. These points have lengths of 16 and 22mm, basal widths of 10 and 13mm, and thickness of 1mm each. Both specimens were recovered with a quantity of fragments from around the fireplace of House 1, indicative of aboriginal manufacture of metal points. The roughness of the form of these artifacts does suggest aboriginal manufacture. It is interesting to note that often the debris from knapping flint is recovered from the fireplaces of prehistoric sites. This evidence suggests that although the material and techniques changed, the locus of manufacturing behavior remained the same.

Lozenge Shaped (Figure 18f-h). Three lozenge shaped points were recovered. Two are iron and one is copper. The copper specimen is probably of aboriginal origin. It has a length of 48mm, a width of 20mm, and a thickness of 1mm. The two iron specimens have lengths of 29 and 31mm, widths of 14 and 16mm and thicknesses of 2mm. Specimen 14160, the larger iron point, is probably of European manufacture. The smaller iron point has a cross-section that suggests that it was made from a broken knifepoint. Both of the apparent aboriginally produced points were from House 1. The presumed European made point was found in House 2. These points show a remarkable similarity with points from the Longest site (*ca.* 1750-1775) (Bell et al., 1967, Figure 48h-n; 54e). Similar points were designated Benton Type A by Harris, et al. (1967:30-2). These points are recovered in quantities on the Southern Plains and are considered to chronologically occur from the mid-18th Century to the mid-19th Century.

Sudbury (1976) using the data from the Deer Creek site in Oklahoma, 34KA3, substantiates this chronological position.

Stemmed Up-Turned Shoulders (Figure 18c and d). Two iron examples of this type were recovered, one from each house. These specimens differ from Stone's (1974:277) stemmed triangular points in two ways: (1) The shoulders on each specimen slant upwards; (2) Both of the points have more elaborated stems than the straight stems exhibited by Stone's (1974, Figure 167e-j). Lengths of the points are 45mm and 55mm and the widths are 21mm and 19mm. The artifacts are too corroded to take measurements of thickness. Krause (1972, Figure 30) reports the presence of points that morphologically and metrically resemble these points. The specimens reported by Krause are from the Leavenworth site (39C09), 1804-1823.

Stemmed Triangular (Figure 18e). Specimen 14118 has been tentatively placed in Stone's (1974:277) defined group, iron stemmed triangular. This single point from House 2 has a stem with a more complex shape than those illustrated by Stone, but the type description permits a lot of variation in stem form. The major disagreement between this point and the stemmed triangular variety is size. By having a length of 60mm, a width of 26mm, and a thickness of 2mm, the Kansas Monument specimen is nearly twice the average size of the points described by Stone.

Fragments. Two fragments were recovered and classified as projectile point fragments. A copper specimen from House 1 is the distal end of a point. It may be from a Lozenge Shaped point or a Benton Type A specimen. An iron fragment from House 2 represents the base of a projectile point. Based on the fragment, the whole point would have been triangular with a concave base.

A number of fragments found around the fireplace of House 1 are interpreted as evidence of projectile point manufacture. The apparent method was to file and bend to break the metal until the point was shaped.

KETTLE PARTS

Kettle Bails (Figure 19b). One complete kettle bail was recovered from House 1. A kettle bail fragment, comprised of one looped end, was found in House 2. Both specimens were made from semicircular pieces of cylindrical iron rod. The complete bail has a length of 41cm from loop midpoint to loop midpoint. Measuring from these midpoints, the kettle or pail to which this bail was attached had a diameter of approximately 34cm. Similar bails were recovered at Fort Michlimackinac (1715-1781) (Stone

1974:171, Figure 92). Bails such as these are derived from copper or brass kettles or pails. The scarcity of brass at the site suggests that these bails were for copper kettles.

Figure 19. Kettle Parts and Miscellaneous: a. Long Iron Awl; b. Kettle Bail; c. Hinge; d. Kettle Lug; e. Buckle Fragment; f. Peened Iron; g. Iron Scraper (?); h. Kettle Rim Fragment.

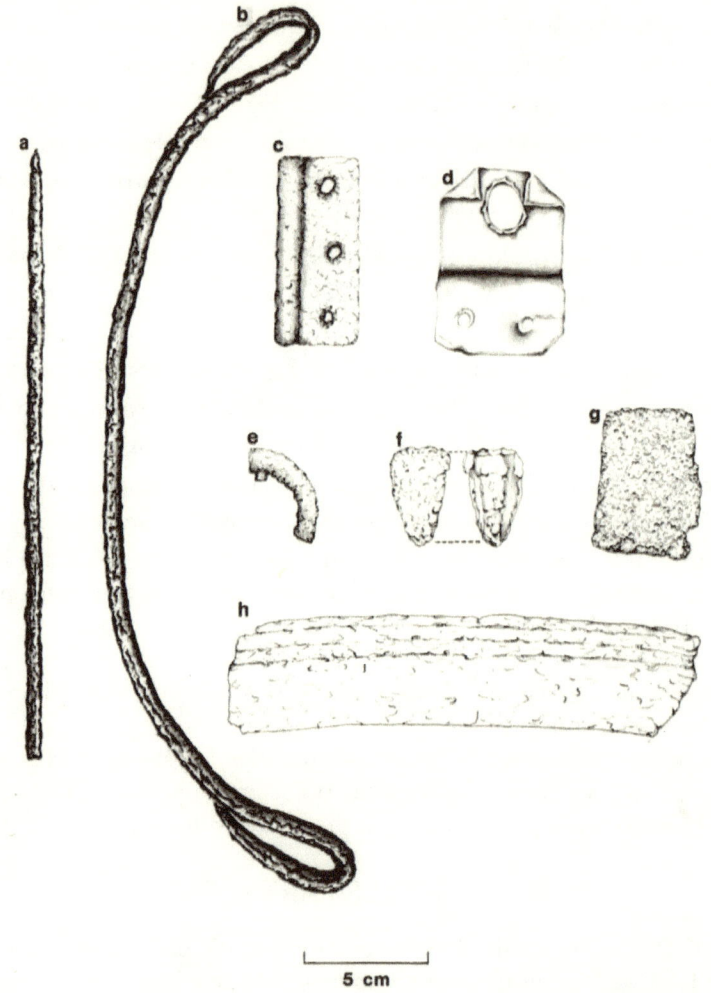

5 cm

Kettle Lugs (Figure 19d). One brass kettle lug was recovered from House 1. The lug was made from a rectangular piece of sheet brass, 1mm thick. The bottom corners were cut off; the upper corners were folded over, a common technique observable on kettle lugs. Two small holes in the lower portion of the lug are for rivets, probably copper. An elongated, large hole in the upper portion is for the bail. The lug was bent or folded at the approximate midpoint of the piece so that when attached to the rim of the kettle the bail would be almost directly over the lip. This lug has a length of 75mm and a width of 51mm. It is almost identical with a specimen from the Gilbert site (*ca.* 1750-1775) (Jelks 1967:105, Figure 46f). The latter site is thought to have received its trade material from the French or Spanish. Wedel describes a similar lug from the Doniphan site, Kansas (14P024) (Wedel 1959:195, Pl. 19b), an early 18th Century Kansa site. This lug also resembles specimens illustrated by Stone (1974, Figure 93); however, all his examples were made from sheet copper.

Kettle Fragments (Figure 19h). Copper kettle fragments were found in both houses. House 1 had only an insignificant amount of small misshapen fragments. Over 95% of the copper fragments, including all the pieces that were cut into strips, were recovered from House 2. The strips ranged in width from 31mm to 43mm, in length from 172mm to approximately 458mm for a folded piece. It is safe to infer that at least one kettle was present in each house. There is a very strong possibility that House 2 had two kettles.

Kettles were very popular in the Indian trade. They may have replaced ceramic vessels or been cut up for use as a raw material. There is still a prevalence of aboriginal pottery suggesting that kettles were not so prevalent as to replace their aboriginal counterparts. It is possible that copper kettles were considered to be more valuable as a source of raw material for projectile points, than for use as a cooking utensil.

AWLS

Two iron awls were recovered. One of these appears to be a fragment; the other is probably a complete specimen.

Long Iron Awl (Figure 19a). This piece differs from all of the examples located in the literature (Stone 1974:155; Krause 1972:71) by being much longer, 248mm (this is twice the size of the largest reported awls), and by having one end that does not taper. The specimen resembles other awls in that it has a square cross-section with a thickness of 12mm and tapers to a point. The blunt end of the piece may be due to modification by the Pawnee.

Small Iron Awl. Smith identified this piece as an awl that is in very poor condition. In its present condition the piece is 93mm long. It has a square cross-section with the center of the shaft having the maximum thickness, 12mm. The piece tapers to a point on both ends. These attributes correspond with Stone's Type I (1974:157) Variety d awls. These awls were almost exclusively associated with the French occupation at Ft.

Michilimackinac (1715-1760). This would indicate a French origin for such awls and an early to mid-18th Century timespan.

NAILS

Two hand-wrought nails were present in the excavated features. Of these two iron specimens, only one is sufficiently well preserved to permit comparisons. This single specimen is an example of the "Type1 Variety a" nail described by Stone (1974:229, 231). As such, it will be described as a member of this type.

Type 1, Variety a (Figure 18k). Nails of this type are rose head nails with pointed shanks. Rose head refers to the marks left by the smith's hammer when the head of the nail is fashioned. This specimen from House 2 is approximately 52mm long (in the range of a two inch nail). The shank is square and tapers from head to point. This type nail is the most common on 18th Century sites (Stone 1974:229).

Unidentified Nail. The unidentified specimen is from Feature 1, the cache pit. The head has been almost completely removed by oxidation, thus prohibiting classification. The shank was square and tapered to a point. This piece may also have been a rose head nail.

ORNAMENTS

This class covers those objects that were used as ornaments by the Pawnee. It is further restricted to only those objects that were meant for personal adornment and does not include those metal pieces adapted to use as ornaments.

Lead Ring (Figure 18i). One example of a lead ring was recovered from House 2. The ring is made from a coiled piece of lead wire with a maximum thickness of 4mm. The wire tapers to a thickness of 2mm on both ends. The outside diameter is 21mm and the inside diameter is 11mm. Such rings are not uncommon as trade goods. Krause (1972:80) reported a similar specimen. Carlson (1972:76, Figure 8A-10) reports a ring made by twisting two coils together at the Linwood site. These rings also occur made out of brass.

Copper Tinklers (Figure 18j). Two copper tinklers were found in the excavations, one from each house. Forming a frustum from a small piece of sheet copper makes a tinkler. It is presumed that the pieces were worn as decoration on clothes. The aboriginals as well as the traders could make tinklers. The specimen from House 1 has a length of 21mm, a width of 7mm and a thickness of .5mm. House 2's specimen is roughly the same in dimensions, but is distorted from being crushed.

Iron Bracelet (Figure 18l). An iron bracelet was recovered from the excavation of Burial 1. The ring is composed of a continuous piece of iron wire 8mm in diameter, formed in an ellipse. The diameter on the longest axis is 86mm, on the short axis 60mm. As was the case with the lead ring, artifacts such as this are not unusual. Similar bracelets can be found made from brass and copper. There are also styles that are more circular than this specimen and others that have a gap purposefully left in the bracelet. Currently such artifacts are not diagnostic of time or origin.

BUCKLES

One iron buckle fragment was recovered from House 1. Since it is in such a fragmentary condition, no attempt is made to classify it as to function or shape. The piece will be considered only as an unidentified buckle.

Buckle (Figure 18e). This single specimen is iron and is in very poor condition. There is a lack of comparative data to ascribe function and the specimen is too incomplete to determine the shape of the frame. It could have been round or D-shaped. The piece is even too corroded to determine cross-section. All that can be reliably stated about the piece is that it had at least one tongue and that the frame had concave sides.

HINGES

As pointed out by Stone (1974:273), hinges can be seen as comprising two groups: structural hinges and furniture hinges. The determination of whether a given specimen is of the structural or furniture variety is often a subjective decision based in part on size and materials of manufacture. The one specimen is considered a structural hinge.

Rectangular Leaf Hinge (Figure 19c). An iron specimen from a test pit in the wheat field south of the part is tentatively placed in Stone's Self-Contained Hinges Type 1 (Stone 1974:217-8). This type refers to rectangular hinges that are composed of three parts: "two iron hinge strap elements, one of which is attached to a movable object...; another element is attached to a stationary object...; the third element is an iron hinge pin which passes between and joins the first two interlocking elements" (Stone 1974:217). The type description is broad enough to include hinges from many parts of the world and many time periods. Thus, to employ this classification does not add anything to the analysis.

The Kansas Monument specimen has a length of 77mm, a width of 33mm, and a thickness at the joining of the two strap elements of 12mm. There are three holes in the piece. The diameter of the holes is 6mm.

Discussion. It is important to note that this piece was recovered from a test pit in the south field. Material that was gathered from this area in a surface collection showed a mixture of artifacts related to the historic

Pawnee settlement and some that could not be associated with this occupation. Included in the latter category are a piece of ironstone bearing the maker's mark of a company that was not founded until 1854 and the trigger guard from a double barrel shotgun, a type not present in this area before the 1850's. Since this field had been under heavy cultivation, it is possible that this piece was intrusive. Without any further data on the test pit and the position of the hinge within it, the true relation of the artifact to the site can remain only speculative.

MISCELLANEOUS

This category is reserved for specimens of unknown function and those fragments that cannot be identified. For those pieces that have a hypothesized identification, a type name is used followed by (?). The remainder of the pieces will be treated as miscellaneous metal pieces.

Peened Iron (Figure 19f). Specimen 14170, recovered from House 2, is a piece of peened iron in the form of a triangle with rounded corners. It has a length of 40mm and a width at the broadest point of 25mm. The face is a convex surface. The concavity of the opposite surface is filled with a quadrangular piece of iron that begins nearly at the vertex with a width of 7mm and expands out to 13mm near the base of the triangle. The metal at the base of the triangle appears to be twisted and jagged, indicating that the piece had an extension or was somehow attached to some other object. The piece may be a gun barrel section or axe blade fragment that was used as a wedge. The convex face is the result of repeated blows by another object.

Iron Scraper (?) (Figure 19g). This artifact from House 2 is a rectangular piece of iron 59mm long and 42mm wide. It is in extremely poor condition. Since the piece is continually splitting along the horizontal plane, it is not possible to make any measurements of thickness. The original account by Smith refers to this piece as a scraper. There is a very slight indication of beveling along two of the sides and, therefore, the scraper designation is allowed to stand. The original source for the iron is open to debate, but a hoe is the most logical candidate.

Miscellaneous Metal Pieces. This category includes material from both houses. House 2, however, on any quantified scale contained the most unidentified metal. Pieces range from small amounts of iron bits to sections of what may be the eye and blade fragments of a hoe. It is impossible to make any attempts to quantify this material because of its deteriorating condition. Counts would be misleading since the material is brittle and, therefore, the number multiplies each time the box they are in is moved. Weight, too, would be misleading for the same reason - as oxidation continues more and more of each artifact is reduced to mere ferric oxide dust.

Included in this category are two pieces of brass, one from each house. These pieces are included in this category because it is not possible to determine whether or not they are fragments from gun, kettle, or other parts. Each piece shows that it has been modified. The common procedure appears to have been to cut or file the piece until it could be worked off by bending and tearing, the same technique used to make projectile points.

GLASS ARTIFACTS

Glass is not a common artifact on early contact sites except in the form of beads. Its scarcity is due in part to its fragileness that made transportation difficult. The fact that whatever goods were transported in glass containers could more efficiently be moved in wooden or metal containers with less breakage and in greater quantity also contributed to glass's scarcity. Some tribes learned to work with glass on their own. They made beads and knapped bits of glass into points and scrapers. At the Kansas Monument site none of these behaviors are in evidence. All glass artifacts are of European manufacture and have not been modified by the Pawnee.

On many historic sites bottles are quite common and can be used to bracket a site in time. Due to considerations noted above, this is not the case at this site. Only a single specimen was recovered. Using Noel Hume's guide (1970:63-8, 71) it is identified as a French wine bottle.

French Wine Bottle (Figure 20). The single bottle specimen was recovered from the northeast side of House 1. The illustration in Figure 20 is based on a reconstruction. The bottle was actually recovered as a mass of fragments. The distortion of the fragments shows the bottle to have partially melted after literally exploding. There is fire-darkening present obscuring the olive green glass color in the area where the bottle burst and melted. The reconstruction is 258mm tall. At the rounded shoulder the outside diameter is 94mm. Then, as is characteristic of French wine bottles, the sides slope gently inward until just before the base they flare out slightly. The base has an outside diameter of 79mm. The interior diameter of the base is 54mm. The kick-up is conical and has a height of 41mm. The orifice has an interior diameter of 19mm and an exterior diameter of 28mm. A pinched rim was applied approximately 3mm below the lip. As can be seen in the illustration, the neck is askew due to the distortion from the explosion.

Figure 20. Reconstruction of a 1770-1785 Period French Wine Bottle.

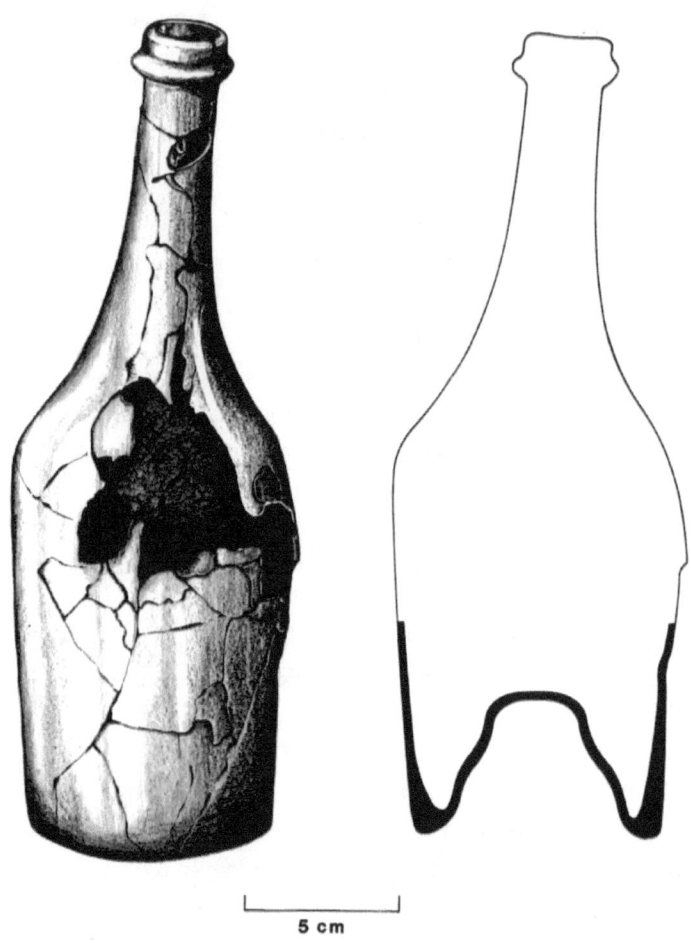

5 cm

The designation of this bottle as a wine bottle does not necessarily imply function. Although at some time it probably did contain wine or some other spirit, bottles such as this also were used to hold gunpowder. As to whether the explosion of the bottle was due to the presence of gunpowder is hypothetical.

The most important aspect of this specimen concerns its manufacture. This bottle is identical to one recovered from a burial at the Utz site in Missouri, 23AD95 (Kay 1968, Pl. 2). Two bottle experts identified the 23AD95 specimen as a French bottle made during the 1770-1785 period

(Kay 1968: 111). The site was likely occupied between 1785 and 1809. This identification supports the early date for the Kansas Monument site.

TRADE BEADS

Trade beads are the most common glass artifacts found on early historic Indian sites. Nancy Fix (1978) studied the beads described below. This section draws heavily on her work. In addition specimens were submitted to Kenneth Kidd, noted bead expert.

The beads are sorted on the basis of the method of manufacture and physical characteristics such as size, shape and color. An attempt to place the beads into the Kidd and Kidd (1970) trade bead classification system proved unsuccessful because that system was designed primarily for beads in the northeast made before 1750 (K. Kidd personal communication). Some tentative dates for the different types were derived through comparisons with Harris and Harris (1967).

All of the specimens examined are of simple construction, meaning they are composed of structurally undifferentiated masses of glass (Harris and Harris 1967:138). It is possible to distinguish between the finishing techniques of the beads: All bugle, or tube-shaped, beads are untumbled; all seed, barrel or donut-shaped, beads are tumbled. Color designations were taken from Kidd and Kidd (1970). Fix (1978:178) compares the Kidds' chart with Bustanoby's (1947), the former standard for color designations.

Lamp Black Bugle Beads (Figure21f). A total of eight opaque lamp black bugle beads were recovered. Three came from the disturbed burial and five from House 2. These untumbled beads have dimensions of 3mm x 7mm. They are tentatively placed in the time bracket 1740-1820.

Figure 21. Trade Beads: a. Translucent Turquoise Seed bead; b. Opaque White Seed Bead; c. Opaque Shadow Blue Seed Bead; d. Opaque White Bugle Bead; f. Lamp Black Bugle Bead.

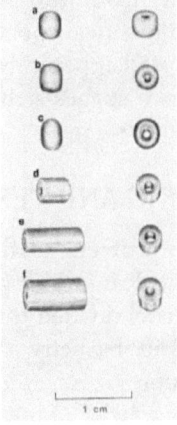

Bright Navy Bugle Bead (Figure21e). A single clear bright navy bugle bead was recovered from House 2. It is untumbled and has dimensions of 3mm x 7.5mm. It is tentatively placed in the time bracket 1740-1820.

Opaque White Bugle Beads (Figure 21d). Forty-six opaque, white bugle beads were recovered. Six came from the disturbed burial and 40 from House 2. These untumbled beads have dimensions of 3mm x 3-4mm. They are tentatively placed in the time bracket 1767-1820.

Opaque White Seed Beads (Figure 21b). A total of 220 opaque white seed beads were recovered. These are the most prevalent beads at the site. One hundred and fifty-two beads were recovered from the disturbed burial. Twelve of these beads were still strung on the original string. Sixty-eight beads came from House 2. These tumbled beads range in dimensions from 3-4mm x 3-4mm. They are tentatively placed in the time bracket 1700-1836.

Translucent Turquoise Seed Beads (Figure 21a). A total of 117 translucent turquoise seed beads were recovered. Eighty-four came from House 2, 33 from the disturbed burial. These tumbled beads have dimensions of 2.5mm x 1.5-2mm. They are tentatively placed in the time bracket 1820-1836.

Opaque Shadow Blue Seed Beads (Figure 21c). Eighty-one opaque shadow blue seed beads were recovered. Four beads came from the disturbed burial, seventy-six from House 2, and one from House 1. These tumbled beads have dimensions of 3-4mm x 2-3mm. They are tentatively placed in the time bracket 1740-1767.

Discussion. It is interesting to note that except for a single bead in House 1, all the beads are from House 2 and Burial 1. Smith (personal communication) reports that the House 2 specimens were found in a mass as if they had been on a crumpled garment.

The date bracket for the Translucent Turquoise Seed Beads indicates that the late date for the site must be considered. However, the dates developed by the Harris's are from the Southern Plains and are only tentative. The author has seen identical specimens from the Hill site, 1775-1815. Stone (1974:111-3) reported apparently similar specimens. Thus, it is a situation in which the evidence suggests that the dates for this particular bead type need to be expanded.

WEAVING AND TEXTILES

As is the case with wooden artifacts, textiles are not well represented in the archaeological record. The Kansas Monument site produced a single representative of this class. Wedel divided these materials into categories of cloth and cordage, matting and basketry (Wedel 1936:90-1). The sole specimen is a fragment of matting.

Matting (Figure 22). A fragment of matting from House 2 was designated Feature 10. It agrees with the description of Pawnee matting presented by Wedel (1936:90-1):

Figure 22. Feature 10, A Preserved Fragment of Matting.

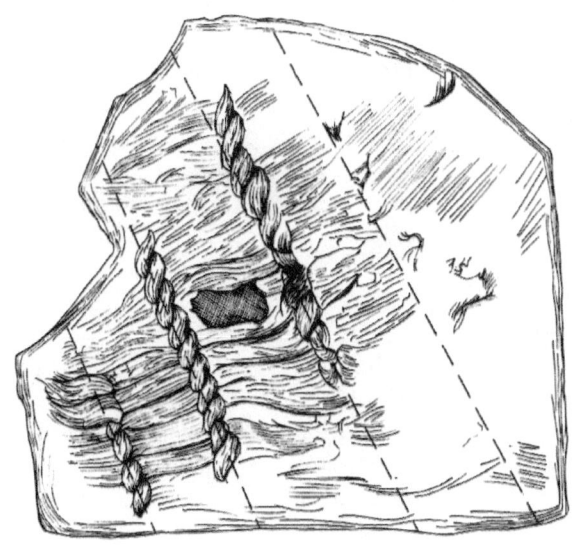

5 cm

All of the specimens are made of some narrow-leaved grass or rush, possibly cattail, and are in simple twined weaving. Each warp element consists of two or more members twisted together into a thick rounded cord; the space between warp elements is generally about one inch. The weft consists of rushes used in pairs; these make a half turn on each other between every two warp elements, one passing on either side of the warp.

The warp elements in this specimen have a diameter of approximately 5mm. The distance between warp elements is approximately 22mm.

As can be seen in Figure 22, this piece of matting was found in association with a surface cache of corn in the east side of House 2. Dunbar (1918:600 as reported in Wedel 1936:91) states that mats were used on the floors, on beds, as curtains to wall off the sleeping compartments, and as wrappings for the dead.

DISCUSSION

The detailed description of the artifact assemblage from an historic Pawnee site fulfills one of the prime goals of this thesis. In addition, the data to test Hypotheses 1, 2, and 4 are presented. The final importance is that the data from which the Pawnee Pattern will be developed in the next chapter is organized.

Hypothesis 1 stated there were two occupations at the site, one early (1750-1800) and one late (1820-30). Using a ceramic seriation and a mean ceramic formula dating system, an early occupation was demonstrated. The trade goods from Houses 1 and 2 supported the early occupation by consistently showing affinities with sites dating between 1750 and 1800. When all factors are considered, an occupation with a midpoint in the 1770's seems most reliable. That such an occupation existed was demonstrated using documentary sources.

Artifact evidence for the late occupation is based solely on the mean ceramic formula dates of the houses. Two houses, 6 and 7, had occupation midpoints of 1825 ± 0, and one, 5, had a midpoint date of 1804 ± 0. However, the remainder of the artifact assemblages from these houses must be examined before a final decision can be made.

One of the prime arguments against two occupations at the site was the lack of evidence for rebuilding of houses. However, the lack of evidence may be the function of an inadequate sample. A conversation by the author with the curator of the museum at the site brought to light some pertinent information. During the construction of the museum's parking lot, the curator, an experienced amateur archaeologist, reports two overlapping lodge circles were plainly evident. Unfortunately, no professional archaeologist was available to verify this occurrence. Thus, further excavation of the site may reveal the sought after evidence for a reoccupation.

The second hypothesis stated that benched houses were late in time. Ceramics constituted the only source that allowed this hypothesis to be tested. Data obtained by the ceramic mean formula do not support this hypothesis.

The fourth hypothesis stated that the inhabitants were in contact with French traders operating out of St. Louis. Consistently, the trade goods from the Kansas Monument site showed affinities with sites south of its position, particularly those in contact with the French. Additionally, the early date for the site suggests that this was the Republican village with which a French trader was licensed by the Spanish government in St. Louis to trade.

This latter point suggests an interesting historical aside. Although St. Louis was under the control of the Spanish, beginning 1770, and the

Spanish licensed the trader, he still used French goods. This implies that the stores of French materials present at the time the Spanish took over were used before Spanish goods were substituted. Economics appear to have overshadowed nationalism.

Houck (1909:268-70) reports the inventory of trade goods present in St. Louis in 1787. Smith (1950a:5-6) compared the Kansas Monument site sample to this list and found of the 24 nonperishable items listed in the inventory, 10 were present. Many of the items present in the inventory but missing from the site, e.g. mirrors, combs, etc. are primarily associated with graves rather than habitation structures. Thus, if undisturbed graves could be located, there might be closer correspondence between the inventory and the site's assemblage.

The next chapter will take the data that have been compiled in the previous pages and develop a Pawnee behavioral model. One of the primary purposes in creating this model, or seriation, will be to help verify statements that were made in this chapter.

5

THE KANSAS MONUMENT SITE IN BROADER PERSPECTIVE

The artifact descriptions above provide a base for a more generalized approach to the study of Pawnee behavioral change. This section is predicated on the assumption that the presence or absence of any given variety of artifact reflects a shift in the behavioral system that utilizes that variety. Drawing on the material previously presented at length, the author seeks to place the Kansas Monument site in a broader perspective by means of a behavioral model, a seriation. Behavioral model and seriation can be used interchangeably because a seriation must model behavioral changes through time in order to be of any use. The seriation as developed in this thesis models the behavioral responses of the Pawnee to a particular set of conditions: the encroachment of Euro-Americans. From this seriation it will be possible not only to arrange Pawnee components in chronological order, but also to draw inferences about the changes that occur through time.

From the standpoint of material culture, there are four ways to view the behavioral interaction between the Pawnee, or any aboriginal population, and Euro-Americans, or any cultural intruders: (1) traditional behaviors can continue, i.e. traditional goods will continue to be manufactured after contact; (2) the aboriginals can copy Euro-American styles or artifacts using native materials, e.g. native clay pipes that are styled like those of the Europeans; (3) Euro-American materials can be adapted to native purposes, e.g. copper or brass kettles can be cut into metal projectile points and scrapers; and (4) traditional artifacts may be abandoned and replaced by Euro-American substitutes or totally new artifacts can enter the system, e.g. iron knives replace stone knives, and guns, which had no aboriginal counterpart, occur. It is these groups, with some modification, that will be used to develop a Pawnee site seriation.

The first group is for traditional artifacts. However, a single grouping of all traditional artifacts would mask certain changes. Familiarity with post-contact Indian sites' material inventories shows that certain types of artifacts are produced for longer periods of time after contact than others. For instance, lithic artifacts cease or decline in production much more quickly than ceramics. The controlling variables may be that one is a male function, the other female. Regardless of reason, such variation should be observable in the model's categories. Therefore, traditional goods are separated into three subcategories: traditional bone, wood, antler, and shell artifacts (i.e. organic artifacts): traditional lithic artifacts; and traditional ceramics, including figurines and other fired clay objects. Since this model is directly based on the Kansas Monument site material, it may need revision to more accurately accommodate additional sites; for instance, the organic category may need to be broken down into its constituent groups: bone, wood, antler, etc.

The second main grouping, but in reality the fourth category, is for those artifacts of native manufacture and raw materials that copy Euro-American artifacts. At the Kansas Monument site this group is composed entirely of locally made gunflints. Other sites may have examples of artifacts such as pipes that copy European styles or pottery which imitates European ceramics. At the Kansas Monument site this is a very small category and it is likely that no site will produce a large number of artifacts in this group. Yet, it is important to note that such artifacts do exist since they reflect a definite impact on traditional concepts and behaviors.

The third main grouping, the fifth category is for those artifacts made from Euro-American materials for aboriginal purposes. This category includes such artifacts as tent pegs made from gun barrels, all metal projectile points and scrapers made from miscellaneous metal pieces. Any Euro-American artifact that is modified from its originally intended purpose belongs in this category. This category should be fairly well represented at those sites where the acculturation process has not yet resulted in the abandonment of traditional behaviors. This category represents the continuation of native behaviors using stronger, possibly more durable, materials. As such, this category represents an interesting point in the acculturation of a native group: traditional materials are abandoned in favor of new raw materials, but traditional styles and types continue. Therefore, it can be inferred the associated behaviors continue also.

The fourth main grouping, the sixth category, includes all Euro-American artifacts that have not been modified by the natives. This category crosscuts all material classes. With the further development of this seriation with the material from other sites it may be deemed necessary to divide this category along raw material lines as was done with the traditional artifacts above. Specimens in this category from the Kansas Monument site are not representative enough of the various raw material classes to make such a division viable.

By dividing the artifact assemblage from an historic site into the groups proposed above, an archaeologist is attaching a special behavioral significance to those artifacts. The model groups represent definable behavior categories for the culture group. To examine the changes between sites through time, the data may be plotted on cumulative frequency graphs, ogives, by converting the raw counts to percentages. When the categories are arranged along the horizontal axis in the sequence they were discussed above, the ogives provide a graphic depiction of temporal change in response to the Euro-American presence. Sites where little or no impact has been made by Euro-Americans will show most of the artifacts to be members of the first three groups. Increasing contact and acculturation will show as increasingly concave lines. A straight line in the final group's column would represent a totally acculturated group, at least acculturated as far as its material culture can indicate.

The material from the Kansas Monument site was divided into the categories just discussed, as can be seen in Table 10. These raw frequency counts were then converted into percentages and graphed in an approach to the study of Pawnee behavioral change. This section is predicated on the assumption that the presence or absence of any given variety of artifact reflects a shift in the behavioral system that utilizes that variety. Drawing on the material previously presented at length, the author seeks to place the

Kansas Monument site in a broader perspective by means of a behavioral model, a seriation. Behavioral model and seriation can be used interchangeably because a seriation must model behavioral changes through time in order to be of any use. The seriation as developed in this thesis models the behavioral responses of the Pawnee to a particular set of conditions: the encroachment of Euro-Americans. From this seriation it will be possible not only to arrange Pawnee components in chronological order, but also to draw inferences about the changes that occur through time.

Table 10. Frequencies of Artifacts in Pawnee Components.

	14RP1	14GE1	25BU1 A	25BU1 B	25BU1 TRANSITIONAL
Organic Aboriginal Artifacts	15	0	17	0	48
Lithic Aboriginal Artifacts	103	32	100	12	49
Ceramic Aboriginal Artifacts	129	13	247	3	941
Aboriginal Copies of Euro-American Artifacts	5	0	0	0	0
Euro-American Artifacts Adapted to Aboriginal Uses	12	0	2	4	2
Euro-American Artifacts	67	10	64	41	48

Included in Table 10 and Figure 23 are the data from the Bogan site (14GE1), a probable Republican Band village, and the Linwood site (25BU1), a multicomponent Grand Band village. It is unfortunate that these are the only historic Pawnee sites for which quantified data were available. The Linwood data were derived from Carlson (1973). The Bogan data were acquired by personal examination of the collection in the Kansas State Historical Society's possession. This small data set allows an examination of the potential usefulness of a behavioral model such as that proposed.

Figure 23. Pawnee Site Seriation: 1. Organic Aboriginal Artifacts; 2. Lithic Aboriginal Artifacts; 3. Ceramic Aboriginal Artifacts; 4. Aboriginal Copies of Euro-American Artifacts; 5. Euro-American Artifacts Adapted to Aboriginal Uses; 6. Euro-American Artifacts.

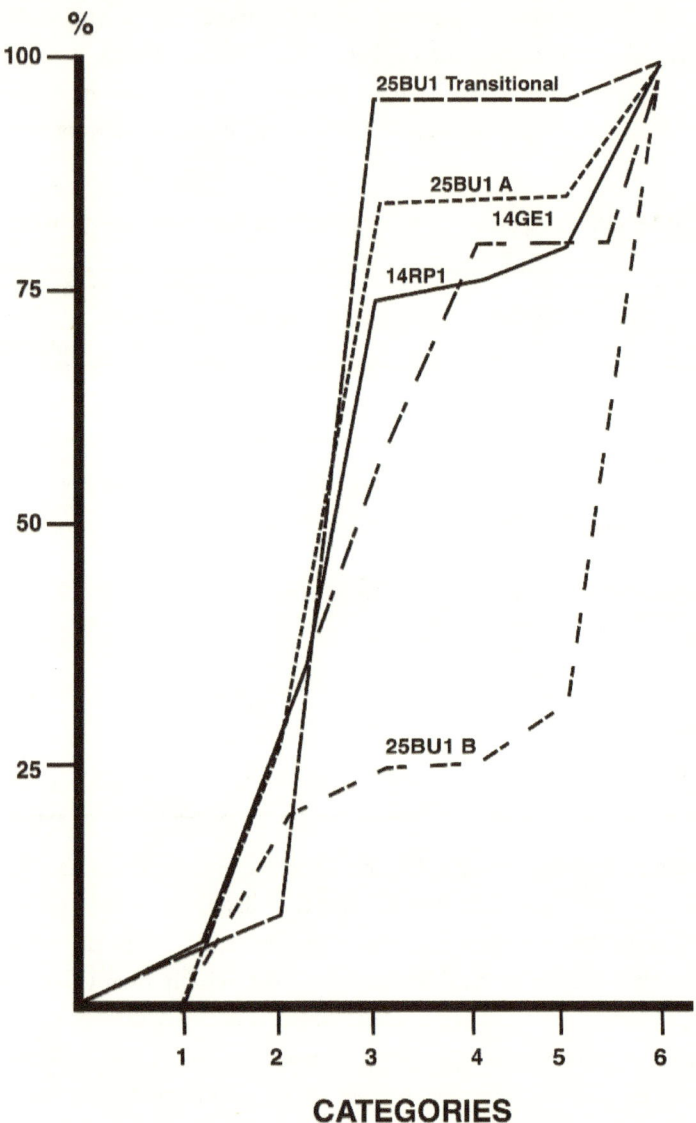

The early and late components of Linwood have strong documentary backing for their proposed time spans. Component A, the early component, was occupied between 1777 and 1809 (Hyde 1974i78; Wedel

1936:17), with a possibility that the occupation began *ca.* 1750 (Carlson 1973:57). Component B, the late component, was occupied between 1851 and 1857 (Wedel 1936:17, 31). Carlson (1973:80) suggests that the "Transitional Component" was occupied somewhere between 1725 and 1775, the time span that marks the transition from Lower Loup to Historic Pawnee.

The categories that comprise this Pawnee behavioral model reflect increasing material culture acculturation, thus they also reflect temporal variability, i.e. the historic record is quite clear that Pawnee acculturation, from both a material and social standpoint, was a long process. Therefore, it should be possible to distinguish graphically between three temporally diverse components such as those at Linwood. Figure 23 illustrates this fact.

If the Kansas Monument site was occupied during the 1770's, as is argued in Chapter 4, then it should be graphically similar to the early component, A, from Linwood. The similarity in graphs may be seen in Figure 23.

An examination of the plots of the Kansas Monument site and the Linwood components allows some inferences to be made about Bogan, an historic Pawnee site of unknown occupation. The lines in the latter half of the graph show distinct separation: Linwood Transitional Component to the top; Linwood B to the bottom; and a cluster composed of the Kansas Monument site, Linwood A, and Bogan occupies the center. However, the graphs over the first three categories do not appear to be quite as distinct as those in the latter half. This apparent mixing of the graphs is actually of great importance.

It was stated earlier that traditional Pawnee behaviors, in regard to tool making, continued for a long time after contact with Euro-Americans. This can be plainly seen in the graph of Linwood B, the late component. What changed through time was the relative percentage of tools in the three aboriginal classes of the pattern, e.g. pottery making continued into the 1850's but was produced in increasingly smaller amounts. Thus, the earliest sites are far richer in pottery than the later ones (Grange 1968:71). As can be seen in Figure 23, the Transitional Component from the Linwood site has the highest percentage of pottery and the late component has the lowest. Then in order come Linwood A, Kansas Monument site and Bogan. This ordering is not contrary to the documentary data that suggest a possible beginning occupation of 1750 for Linwood A (Carlson 1973:57).

Based on the graphs, Bogan would appear to be a late 18th Century occupation. This date is derived from the overlap in occupations between Linwood A and the Kansas Monument site. Hyde (1974:132-3) states a Republican Pawnee village on the Republican River in 1798 was attacked and burned by the Omaha. Marshall and Witty (1967:19) in their report on

Bogan suggest that it was occupied for a short period of time and then abandoned after it was burned. There was no direct evidence that the site was burned by enemy action, but it was a fortified site indicating that the Pawnee anticipated hostile contact. The main problem with trying to identify the Bogan site with the one in the documentary account is its position: It is unlikely that the Omaha penetrated so far south into Kansas. Thus, the situation is that on the one hand Bogan was a defensively built village that was burned and was probably occupied during the last part of the 18th Century. On the other hand, the documentary accounts of a village that matches this description would seem to indicate a village farther north up the Republican River valley. Also of importance to this discussion is the sample size: The Bogan collection is the smallest of the five, only 55 specimens. This small sample size may affect the position of Bogan in relation to the other sites. Thus, as in so many archaeological problems, the final resolution of the chronological placement for Bogan rests in the acquisition of further data through excavation.

The graph of Linwood A has been interpreted as evidence that the Grand occupation of the site began *ca.* 1750 and was thus earlier than the initial occupation at the Kansas Monument site. This is a reasonable interpretation and explanation of the data. However, consideration must be given to an explanation of the variability between the graphs if one accepts only the 1777-1809 date bracket for Linwood A. Such an explanation has direct implications for Hypothesis 4 of this thesis.

Hypothesis 4 stated that the Republican River valley was a preferred trade area and that trade influenced the periodic reoccupation of the area. The test implication for this hypothesis: Given two Republican Band sites of comparable time depth, one on the Republican River and one on the Platte, the only other known area of occupation for this band, the site on the Republican should show a higher incidence of trade goods. Unfortunately, the Linwood site is a Pawnee Grand Band village rather than a Pawnee Republican Band village. This does not necessarily negate the possibility of testing this hypothesis for two reasons: (1) Just a few miles west of Linwood is the Savannah site, a Republican village occupied during the third quarter of the 18th Century (Brown 1892, in Hyde 1974:126-7); (2) The Grand were very jealous of their trade relations with the French and positioned themselves on the Platte so as to control the traders passing them and reaching the other groups. In this way, the other Pawnee bands' villages, particularly those of the Skidi band, were forced to either trade with the Grand rather than the French or to select from already picked over goods. Thus, a Grand site on the Platte would have a greater incidence of trade material than any other band's village on the river since the other bands were dependent on the Grand for trade. Therefore, if the Republican River valley afforded greater trade opportunities to the Republican Band than did the Platte, one would expect a Republican site on the Republican River to be similar to a Grand site on the Platte. As can be seen in Figure 23, the Kansas Monument site actually has a higher incidence of trade material than Linwood A, which suggests that the Republican River valley was a beneficial trade area for the Republican Band. The best test for this hypothesis would be a comparison between the Savannah site and the Kansas Monument site. As this cannot currently be accomplished, one can only assume that the Savannah site being west of Linwood, and thus subject to the Grand Band's control of trade, would not show a greater degree of material culture acculturation than Linwood.

The fact that Linwood A has fewer trade goods than Kansas Monument site does not mean that trade on the Republican was better than trade on the Platte, per se. There are two additional factors that affect the composition of Linwood's material culture inventory: 1. Although the Grand Band at the Linwood site controlled the trade with the villages west of their location, they were themselves only second in line in access to the French traders' goods. An Oto village was the first village on the Platte that the French traders came to as they moved up the river. Since the Oto were better supplied with firearms than the Grand and had a longstanding trade relationship with the French, they were unhampered by the Pawnee and thus exercised first choice over the goods carried by the traders. The goods that reached the Grand were reduced in quantity and quality, which could account for the low incidence of trade material at Linwood A (Hyde 1974: 128). 2. It has been demonstrated at Canadian sites that when a tribal group acted as a middle man between white traders and other groups, the middle man group will show a much lower incidence of trade material than the groups with which they are trading (Ray 1978:31-4). It is doubtful that the Grand traded away the majority of the goods they acquired from the French for the simple reason that they primarily traded with the Skidi who were usually hostile towards them. In addition the Grand charged extremely high prices for their goods, thus limiting economically the amount of trade goods any other group could acquire. Therefore, the Grand would have retained sufficient goods such as firearms, etc. to protect themselves and they would have also maintained an inventory of goods that the other groups could not afford. Also, the Canadian groups studied by Ray (1978) had a different trade network operating than that seen here: The Canadian groups emphasized trade whereas the Grand, when they were in the mood, stopped trade with the Skidi altogether. Assuming the samples are not biased, it is proposed that a combination of the above two factors account for the variation between the graphs of Kansas Monument site and Linwood A. These two factors would affect the graph of Linwood A regardless of its temporal position, but the affect would be more noticeable if the late occupation is accepted rather than the proposed early dates.

What has become apparent in this discussion is that this Pawnee site seriation can be useful in archaeological studies. Equally apparent is the fact that the graphs must be looked at as a whole. If the last three categories account for over 50% of the total, then particular attention must be paid to the behavior of the lines over the first three categories. The reverse of this also holds true.

An important point is the ease with which graphs such as these could be distorted. If raw count data were entered for miscellaneous metal pieces or non-utilized flakes, these percentages for the various groups would be seriously altered. Rather than allow this to happen, counts based on location were used for the unidentifiable/unused artifacts, i.e. each occurrence of a type of metal, chert, stone, etc. is counted as one regardless of the number of pieces present. This method reflects the degree of popularity of any given metal, etc. since it counts the loci of occurrence throughout the site. At the same time, this method does not allow metal pieces to skew the counts because of their continued oxidation that causes the specimens to break into smaller pieces, thus continuously increasing the raw count.

All the preceding statements about the Pawnee seriation and the information it contains were derived from visual inspections of the graphs. Since the model is based on numerical relationships, there should be a mathematical justification of the inferences that were made. Towards this end, the pattern data were subjected to a cluster analysis, BMDP2M (Dixon 1975:323-37), using the chi-square procedure. Table 11 and Table 12 show the results of the cluster analysis.

Table 11. Cluster Analysis Results Dendrogram Using the Pawnee Site Seriation Data.

Amalgamation Distance	14RP1	14GE1	25BU1 A	25BU1 B	25BU1 TRANSITIONAL
4.279					
6.692					
10.187					
20.973					

Table 12. Initial Distances Among Cases.

	14RP1	14GE1	25BU1 A	25BU1 B	25BU1 TRANSITIONAL
14RP1	0.00	4.28	6.10	8.17	19.21
14GE1	4.28	0.18	5.92	6.17	16.12
25BU1 A	6.10	5.92	0.29	10.85	13.81
25BU1 B	8.17	6.17	10.85	0.15	20.49
25GU1 TRANSITIONAL	19.21	16.12	13.81	20.49	0.47

It can be clearly seen that Kansas Monument Site, Bogan, and Linwood A are closer to each other than to either Linwood B or the Transitional Component. Also, it can be seen that Linwood B and the Transitional Component are as far from each other as they are from the other sites and components.

It is interesting to note that the Transitional Component from Linwood has the largest initial distance measurements of all the cases. These large measures are indicative of the fact that this component is very early in the sequence. The remainder of the sites and components reflect a culture that is already being dramatically affected by Euro-American contact. The Transitional Component was a culture that, materially, was just beginning to be acculturated.

DISCUSSION

Many pages in this thesis are devoted to expounding nomothetic goals for archaeology and the relevance of quantification studies to obtaining these goals. Yet, it is an undeniable fact that the results of the research herein reported are predominantly particularistic. The Pawnee behavioral model is useful for chronological placement of sites and the making of general statements about material culture acculturation. These are particularistic objectives, but they are particularistic objectives integral to the development of general laws of behavior.

In constructing the model several things were alluded to. It was noted that tools associated with male behaviors appeared to have been replaced by Euro-American substitutes more quickly than were female-used tools. This suggests differential interaction of the sexes with traders, although Weltfish (1965:145-6) notes that in the mid-19th Century both sexes dealt with traders. It may be that females entered the trade picture at a slower rate than males or that they selected for trade items of a more perishable nature or items that were not tools, i.e. cloth, beads, etc. It was further noted that tools that were essential to acquiring the items the traders desired, were replaced first. The model also can be used to discuss the importance of trade in the settlement behavior of the Pawnee. These are the sorts of particularistic facts necessary to the construction of general laws of human behavior. One cannot meet a nomothetic goal without satisfying the particularistic requirements that form the basis for general laws.

The largest problem that must be surmounted in order to utilize the model to its fullest nomothetic potential is the lack of data. Only general classes could be used because there were insufficient amounts of data. Ideally, the behavioral categories would be broken down into the constituent artifact types, arranged in a permanent, predetermined fashion. Each component would have its assemblage placed in this model. Comparisons could then be made between components of both similar and different ages. In this way, an archaeologist can see the specific changes occurring among the components. It is through the explanation of these changes that the nomothetic goals of archaeology will be met.

A strength of the seriation is its across the board applicability. It was developed for a Pawnee Republican Band village site. Yet, it was used to compare that site with a Pawnee Grand Band village. It is the author's belief that the model has applicability beyond this. It should be possible, particularly on the general level as used in this thesis, to compare different cultural groups. With certain modifications to the specific artifact types, it should be possible to compare different cultural groups through the use of the model in its expanded, constituent artifact form.

This means it will be possible to examine concurrent changes among different cultural groups and also to compare the changes within those groups through time. To the author, it is this potential for the use of the model that holds the greatest prospects for not just Pawnee archaeology but all historic Indian archaeology.

6

SUMMARY AND CONCLUSIONS

It has been the endeavor of this thesis to present as complete a picture of an excavated historic Pawnee site as the author felt possible. Each section has been designed so as not only to further the understanding of the Kansas Monument site but also to contribute towards our understanding of the Pawnee and the changes that tribe experienced through time. In total, this thesis not only contributes to Pawnee culture history but also argues for historical archaeology as a science directly concerned with post-contact aboriginal sites. As such, this work has gone beyond being an extension of history but has approached the problems it sought to solve with an archaeological perspective. History and archaeology were combined to produce a work which transcends that which could be produced using either alone.

The author has produced as detailed an account of the material culture as is necessary to support this thesis. Beyond mere description, the accounts of each artifact type made comparisons with other sites and drew conclusions in regard to place of origin, age, and affect on native culture. With more work in this area, it is predicted that a clear and precise picture of Euro-American trade patterns and the affects of this trade on native material culture will emerge.

Drawing on the data presented in the previous chapters, with the assumption that sample bias is not involved, the following picture of the site can be developed: The Kansas Monument site was a Republican Pawnee site occupied during the 1770's. The Pawnee carried on a lucrative trade with French traders out of St. Louis. Due in part to this trade and their occupation of the Republican River valley, this band of the Pawnee was forced to protect themselves from hostile groups such as the Kansa and Osage. Thus, the village was built in a defensive fashion on a bluff top with a fortification wall. Trade on the Republican River was better than on the Platte River since they were not forced to deal with the Grand Band or to settle for goods already picked over by the Oto. The richness of trade coupled with the natural abundance of game and the excellent farmland in the valley probably helped draw the band back each time it was driven off from the river valley. The presence of Euro-American goods was already having an affect on the native behaviors. Certain traditional goods, such as finely-knapped pieces, were no longer in production, apparently replaced by Euro-American goods. Those aboriginal tools still being produced such as bone agricultural implements, heavy stone hide working tools, and pottery are all associated with female activities. Shaft polishers and whetstones, which were useful to males in getting full benefit from their metal tools, were also still produced.

The houses in which the inhabitants lived were both benched and unbenched. Persons of high status occupied specially prepared houses with burned clay floors, eight center posts, and a buffalo skull shrine. These same persons appear to have had a greater access to trade goods than those who did not live in the special houses. These persons may have been the superlative hunters of the group and thus able to secure more of the hides that the traders desired than the average hunter.

The village was not occupied very long and was abandoned sometime before the turn of the century. An attack by hostiles may have been responsible for the abandonment. Depending upon when the village was abandoned and the reasons behind it, the band may have sought refuge on the Platte or at the Hill site. In between the time that the Kansas Monument site was abandoned and the time of its possible reoccupation in the 1820's it is postulated that the Bogan site was occupied. This occupation was very short lived and ended as a result of hostile action, possibly a raid by the Omaha in 1798.

During the 1820's the Kansas Monument site may have been reoccupied. It is thus possible that this was the village visited by Jedediah

Smith in 1826. The village was definitely not the one visited by Lt. Pike in 1806 and was most likely not even occupied at that time.

The above paragraphs present as clear a picture of the occupation at the Kansas Monument site as the author can derive from the data. This picture provides several avenues of research for the future of Pawnee archaeology: (1) It is hypothesized that among the Pawnee those tools associated with female behaviors, e.g. agriculture, etc., were replaced with Euro-American substitutes at a much slower rate than male used tools; (2) Those tools that are directly related to the acquisition of those goods in which the traders were interested, e.g. hunting tools, were replaced with superior Euro-American tools first; (3) Because the traders were dealing in furs, the material culture inventory variation between the superlative hunter and the average hunter becomes very marked; (4) Because furs were the main trade items, as trade goods became more important to the group for its existence, the evidence for processing furs should also increase in the archaeological picture.

It has also been demonstrated that Grange's ceramic mean date formula system is a very valuable tool in Pawnee and Lower Loup studies. The seriation he developed does require modification of the historic Pawnee portion but is considered to be basically accurate aside from that.

Another area of study that may be of importance in the future is the relationship between pottery rim decoration and the Pawnee bands. The Kansas Monument site ceramic assemblage showed that rim motifs might be useful in distinguishing between bands. A large-scale study of this possibility is currently being developed by Grange, and may possibly turn out to be the greatest contribution to Pawnee archaeology since Pawnee and Lower Loup Pottery.

By drawing on the data that reflect the behavioral response of the Pawnee to the presence of Euro-Americans, it was possible to develop a seriation. Because the seriation was based upon material culture acculturation, the aforementioned behavioral response, it was possible not only to demonstrate that the Kansas Monument site was a very early site, but also to suggest explanations for the variations between components visible in the model.

The significance of identifying the site as an early historic site is great. Of prime importance is the fact that this site dates from the period when the Republican band was becoming distinct from the other three Pawnee bands. The earliest reference to the Republicans is 1775 (Barry 1961: 203). Therefore, it is believed that the differentiation of the Republican band took place around the third quarter of the 18th Century (Grange 1968:119). Through the use of the pattern, the Kansas Monument site has been shown to represent the earliest known Republican band site. Its dates have been pushed back to the earliest part of the sequence for Republican bands. Through the study of sites such as this, archaeologists will be able to examine the factors that affected differentiation and how the separate bands developed. It is the author's belief that this study of the Kansas Monument site has laid the foundation for such a study.

REFERENCES CITED

Barry, Louise 1961

Kansas Before 1854: A Revised Annals, *The Kansas Historical Quarterly*, Vol. 27, No. 2, pp. 201-219, Topeka.

Bell, R. E., E. B. Jelks, W. W. Newcomb 1967

A *Pilot Study of Wichita Indian Archaeology and Ethnohistory*. Final Report to the National Science Foundation, Grant GS-964.

Birkby, W. H. 1962

Additional Data on the Kansas Monument Site. MS on file Museum of Anthropology, University of Kansas, Lawrence, Kansas.

Blaine, J. C. and R. K. Harris 1967

Guns In The Gilbert Site, ed. by E. B. Jelks, The *Bulletin of the Texas Archaeological Society*, vol. 37, pp. 33-86. Austin.

Bouchard, Russel 1976

Les Armes de Traites. *Collection Histoire Populaire du Quebec*, No. 3. Les Editions du Boreal Express, Sillery, Quebec.

Bradbury, J. 1819

Travels in the Interior of America in the Years 1809, 1810, 1811. Vol. V, Reuben Thwaites, ed. *Early Western Travels, 1748-1846*. A. H. Clark, Cleveland.

Brown, G. L. 1892

The History of Butler County, 1876. *Transactions and Reports of the Nebraska State Historical Society*, Vol. 4, pp. 275-305. Lincoln.

Bustanoby, J. H. 1947

Principles of Color Mixing. Reed Publishing Company. New York.

Carlson, G. F. 1973

Archaeological Salvage and Survey in Nebraska: Highway Archaeological and Historical Salvage Investigations in Nebraska, 1965 to 1968. *Nebraska State Historical Society Publications in Anthropology*, Number 5. Lincoln.

Chapman, Carl 1959

The Little Osage and Missouri Indian Village Sites *Ca.* 1727-1777 A.D. *The Missouri Archaeologist*, Vol. 21, No. 1. Columbia.

Deetz, James and Edwin Dethlefsen 1965

The Doppler Effect and Archaeology: A Consideration of the Spatial Aspects of Seriation. *Southwestern Journal of Anthropology*, Vol. 21, pp. 196-206. Albuquerque.

Dixon, W.J. 1975

BMDP Biomedical Computer Programs. University of California Press, Berkeley.

Dollar, C. D. 1968

Some Thoughts on Theory and Method in Historical Archaeology. *The Conference on Historic Sites.* Archaeology Papers edited by Stanley South, Vol. 2, pt. 2, pp. 3-34. Raleigh, N. C.

Doran, J. E. and F. R. Hodson 1975

Mathematics and Computers in Archaeology. Harvard University Press. Cambridge.

Dunbar, J. B. 1908

The White Man's Foot in Kansas. Kansas State Historical Society, State Printing Office. Topeka.

Fix, N. J. 1978

Glass Beads. In, The Talking Crow Site by C. S. Smith. *University of Kansas Publications in Anthropology*, Number 9. Lawrence, Kansas.

Flannery, K. V. 1973

Archaeology with a Capital "S". In, *Research and Theory in Current Archaeology*, ed. by C. L. Redman, pp. 47-53. Wiley-Interscience, New York.

Fogel, R. W. and S. L. Engerman 1974

Time on the Cross. Little, Brown and Co., New York.

Fontana, B. L. 1965

On the Meaning of Historic Sites Archaeology. *American Antiquity*, Vol. 31, No. 1, pp. 61-5. Menasha.

Ford, J. A. 1949

Cultural Dating of Prehistoric Sites in the Viru Valley, Peru. In "Surface Survey of the Viru Valley, Peru," by J. A. Ford and G. R. Willey. *Anthropological Papers of the American Museum of Natural History*, Vol. 43, pt. 1, pp. 29-87. New York.

Good, M. E. 1972

Guebert Site: an 18th Century Historic Kaskaskia Indian Village. *The Central Archaeological Societies, Inc. Memoir II*. Wood River, 111.

Grange, R. T. 1968

Pawnee and Lower Loup Pottery. *Nebraska State Historical Society Publications in Anthropology*, No. 3. Lincoln.

Grange, R. T. 1974

Pawnee Potsherds Revisited: Formula Dating of a Non-European Ceramic Tradition. In, *The Conference on Historic Sites Archaeology Papers*, 1972. Ed. by Stanley South, pp. 318-36. Columbia, South Carolina.

Grange, R. T. 1977

Cumulative Seriation and Ceramic Formula Dating: A Preliminary Survey. *History and Archaeology*, No. 16. Parks Canada, Ottawa.

Grinnell, G. B. 1893

Pawnee Hero Stories and Folk Tales. Scribner's, New York.

Hagerty, Gilbert. 1963

The Iron Trade Knife in Oneida Territory. *Pennsylvania Archaeologist*, Vol. XXXIII, pp. 93-114.

Hamilton, T. M. 1960

Indian Trade Guns. *The Missouri Archaeologist*, Vol. 22. Columbia.

Hamilton, T. M. 1968

Early Indian Trade Guns: 125-1775. *Contributions of the Museum of the Great Plains,* Number 3. Lawton, Oklahoma.

Hanson, C. E. 1956

The Northwest Gun. *Nebraska State Historical Society Publications in Anthropology*, No. 2. Lincoln.

Harris, R. K. and I. M. Harris 1967

Trade Beads, Projectile Points, and Knives. In, *A Pilot Study of Wichita Indian Archaeology and Ethnohistory*, ed. by R. E. Bell, E. B. Jelks, and W. W. Newcomb. Final Report to the National Science Foundation, Grant GS-964.

Harris, R. K., I. M. Harris, J. C. Blaine, and J. Blaine 1965

A Preliminary Archaeological and Documentary Study of the Womack Site, Lamar County, Texas. *Bulletin of the Texas Archaeological Society*, Vol. 36, pp. 287-364. Texas Archaeological Society, Austin.

Harris, R. K., I. M. Harris, and J. N. Woodall 1967

Tools. In, The Gilbert Site, ed. by E. B. Jelks. *Bulletin of the Texas Archaeological Society*, Vol. 37, pp. 188-190. Dallas.

Harris, R. K. and C. D. Tunnell 1967

Miscellaneous European Goods. In, The Gilbert Site, ed. by E. B. Jelks, *The Bulletin of the Texas Archaeological Society*, Vol. 37, pp. 105-111. Austin.

Hayward, J. F. 1963

The Art of the Gunmaker, Vol. II. St. Martins Press.

Hill, A. T. 1927

Mr. A. T. Hill's Own Story. *Nebraska History Magazine*, Vol. X, No. 3, pp. 162-167. Lincoln.

Holder, Preston 1970

The Hoe and the Horse on the Plains. University of Nebraska Press, Lincoln.

Houch, Louis 1909

The Spanish Regime in Missouri. 2 vols. Chicago.

Hyde, G. E. 1974

The Pawnee Indians. University of Oklahoma Press, Norman.

Irving, J. T., Jr. 1835

Indian Sketches. Privately printed, London.

Jelks, E. B. 1967

The Gilbert Site. *The Bulletin of the Texas Archaeological Society*, Vol. 37. Austin.

Kay, Marvin 1968

Two Historic Indian Burials from an Open Site, 23AD95, Adair County, Missouri. *Plains Anthropologist*, Vol. 13, No. 40, pp. 103-115. Lincoln.

Kidd, K. E. and M. A. Kidd 1970

A Classification System for Glass Beads for the Use of Field Archaeologists. *Canadian Historical Sites; Occasional Papers in Archaeology and History*, No. 1, pp. 45-89. Ottawa.

Krause, R. A. 1972

The Leavenworth Site: Archaeology of an Historic Arikara Community. *University of Kansas Publications in Anthropology*, No. 3. Lawrence, Kansas.

Lehmer, D. J. 1971

Introduction to Middle Missouri Archaeology. *Anthropological Papers* 1, National Park Service, Washington, D. C.

Leone, Mark 1972

Issues in Anthropological Archaeology. In *Contemporary Archaeology*, ed. by Mark Leone, pp. 14-27. Southern Illinois University Press, Carbondale, Illinois.

Marshall, J. O. and T. A. Witty, Jr. 1967

The Bogan Site, 14GE1, An Historic Pawnee Village. MS on file Kansas State Historical Society, Topeka.

Maxwell, M. S. and L. H. Binford 1961

Excavation at Fort Michilimackinac, Mackinac City, Michigan: 1959 Season. *Michigan State University, Cultural Series*, Vol. 1, No. 1. Lansing.

Meighan, C. W. 1959

A New Method for the Seriation of Archaeological Collections. *American Antiquity*, Vol. 25, No. 1, pp. 203-11. Salt Lake City.

Miroir, M. P., R. K. Harris, J. C. Blaine, Janson McNay, D. C. Book, Floyd Cigainero, Roger McNay, J. B. Raffaelli, Jr. and P. E. Schoen 1975

Bernard de la Harpe and the Nassonite Post. *Bulletin of the Texas Archaeological Society*, Vol. 44, pp. 113-169. Austin.

Moorehouse, George 1927

The Case for Kansas. *Nebraska History Magazine*, Vol. X, No. 3, pp. 226-254. Lincoln.

Munday, F. J. 1927

Pike-Pawnee Village Site. *Nebraska History Magazine*, Vol. X, No. 3, pp. 168-92. Lincoln.

Nasatir, A. P. 1952

Before Lewis and Clark: Documents Illustrating the History of the Missouri, 1785 to 1804. 2 vols., St. Louis Historical Document Foundation, St. Louis.

Neitzel, R. S. 1965

Archaeology of the Fatherland Site: The Grand Village of the Natchez. *Anthropological Papers of the American Museum of Natural History*, New York.

Nie, N. H., C. H. Hull, J. G. Jenkins, Karin Steinbrenner, and D. H. Bent 1975

Statistical Package for the Social Sciences. 2nd Edition. McGraw-Hill, New York.

Noel Hume, Ivor 1969

Historic Archaeology. Alfred Knopf, New York.

Noel Hume, Ivor 1970

Guide to Artifacts of Colonial America. Knopf, New York.

Noel Hume, Ivor 1974

All the Best Rubbish. Harper and Row, New York.

Otto, J. S. 1977

Artifacts and Status Differences—A Comparison of Ceramics from Planter, Overseer, and Slave Sites on an Antebellum Plantation. In, *Research Strategies in Historical Archaeology*, ed. by Stanley South, pp. 91-118. Academic Press, New York.

Peterson, H. I. 1965

American Indian Tomahawks. *Contributions from the Museum of the American Indian*, Vol. XIX.

Quimby, G. I. 1966

Indian Culture and European Trade Goods. University of Wisconsin Press, Madison.

Ray, A. J. 1978

History and Archaeology of the Northern Fur Trade. *American Antiquity*, Vol. 43, No. 1, pp. 26-34. Washington, D. C.

Russell, C. P. 1962

Guns on the Early Frontier. University of California Press, Los Angeles.

Russell, C. P. 1967

Firearms, Traps, and Tools of the Mountain Men. Alfred Knopf, New York.

Schuyler, R. L. 1970

Historical and Historic Sites Archaeology as Anthropology: Basic Definitions and Relationships. *Historical Archaeology*, Vol. IV, pp. 83-89. Moravian College, Bethlehem, Pennsylvania.

Secoy, F. R. 1953

Changing Military Patterns on the Great Plains. *Monographs of the American Ethnological Society*, Number 21. J. J. Augustin, Locust Valley, New York.

Shaeffer, J. B. 1958

The Alibates Flint Quarry, Texas. *American Antiquity*, Vol. 24, No. 2.

Sheldon, A. E., ed. 1927

The War Between Nebraska and Kansas. *Nebraska History Magazine*, Vol. X, No. 3. Lincoln.

Shepard, A. O. 1956

Ceramics for the Archaeologist. Publication 609, Carnegie Institution of Washington, Washington, D. C.

Smith, C. S. 1949

Fieldwork in Kansas, 1949. *Plains Archaeological Conference News Letter*, Vol. 2, No. 4, pp. 5-6. Lincoln.

Smith, C. S. 1950a

European Trade Material from the Kansas Monument Site. *Plains Archaeological Conference News Letter*, Vol. 3, pp. 2-9. Lincoln.

Smith, C. S. 1950b

The Pottery from the Kansas Monument Site. *Plains Archaeological Conference News Letter*, Vol. 3, No. 4, pp. 7-9. Lincoln.

Smith, C. S. 1960

Manufacture of Gunflints in France. In, Indian Trade Guns, ed. by T. M. Hamilton, *The Missouri Archaeologist*, Vol. 22, pp. 40-49. Columbia.

South, Stanley 1972

Evolution and Horizon as Revealed in Ceramic Analysis in Historical Archaeology. *The Conference on Historic Site Archaeology Papers, 1971*, Vol. 6, Pt. 2, pp. 71-116. The Institute of Archaeology and Anthropology, University of South Carolina, Columbia.

South, Stanley 1977

Method and Theory in *Historical Archaeology*. Academic Press, New York.

Stone, L. M. 1974

Fort Michilimackinac 1715-1781. *Publications of the Museum, Michigan State University, Anthropological Series*, Vol. 2. Lansing.

Strong, W. D. 1935

An Introduction to Nebraska Archaeology. *Smithsonian Miscellaneous Collections*, Vol. 93, No. 10. Washington, D. C.

Sudbury, Byron 1976

Ka-3, The Deer Creek Site—An Eighteenth Century French Contact Site in Kay County, Oklahoma. *Bulletin of the Oklahoma Anthropological Society*, Vol. 24, pp. 1-136. Oklahoma City.

Tolsted, Laura and Ada Swineford 1957

Kansas Rocks and Minerals. Kansas Geological Survey, Lawrence, Kansas.

Walker, I. C. 1967

Historic Archaeology—Methods and Principles. *Historical Archaeology.* Vol. I. pp. 23-34. Wayne State University, Detroit, Michigan.

Wedel, M. M. 1976

Ethnohistory: Its Payoffs and Pitfalls for Iowa Archaeologists. *Journal of the Iowa Archaeological Society*, Vol. 23, pp. 1-44.

Wedel, W. R. 1936

An Introduction to Pawnee Archaeology. *Bureau of American Ethnology Bulletin 112.* Washington, D. C.

Wedel, W. R. 1938

The Direct Historical Approach in Pawnee Archaeology. *Smithsonian Miscellaneous Collections*, Vol. 97, No. 7, Washington, D. C.

Wedel, W. R. 1959

An Introduction to Kansas Archaeology. *Bureau of American Ethnology Bulletin 174*, Washington, D. C.

Wedel, W. R. 1961

Prehistoric Man on the Great Plains. University of Oklahoma Press, Norman.

Weltfish, Gene 1965

The Lost Universe. University of Nebraska, Lincoln.

White, Leslie 1938

Science is Sciencing. *Philosophy of Science*, Vol. 5, pp. 369-89.

Witty, T. A. 1967

1966 Excavations at the Kansas Monument Site, 14RP1. *Plains Anthropologist.* Vol. 12, No. 36, p. 218. Lincoln.

Witty, T. A. 1968

The Pawnee Indian Village Museum Project. *Kansas Anthropological Association Newsletter*, Vol. 13, No. 5, pp. 1-5. Topeka.

Woodward, Arthur 1946

The Metal Tomahawk; Its Evolution and Distribution in the North Ameri*ca. Ticonderoga Museum Bulletin*, Vol. VII, No. 3.

Woodward, Arthur 1965

Indian Trade Goods. *Oregon Archaeological Society Publication*, No. 2, 1965.

Woodward, Arthur 1970

Denominators of the Fur Trade. Socio-Technical Publications, Pasadena.

Pawnee Indian Village Museum

ABOUT THE AUTHOR

Rick Roberts earned a MA, M.Phil. and Ph.D. in anthropology from the University of Kansas. After 10 years as a professional archaeologist, he joined the U.S. Foreign Service and spent 28 years doing applied anthropology as a diplomat in American embassies, primarily in the Middle East. His last two overseas assignments were in Iraq where he led a Provincial Reconstruction Team, which included helping to preserve historic Babylon and other Iraqi cultural heritage sites. Since retiring in 2013, Rick has returned to his archaeological roots and plans to produce a series of popular archaeology books. He is married and lives in Oklahoma City.

Rick Roberts in Historic Babylon

www.ingramcontent.com/pod-product-compliance
Lightning Source LLC
Chambersburg PA
CBHW020532290526
45786CB00002B/834